The Great Plague and Fire of London

The Great Plague and Fire of London

Charles J. Shields

CHELSEA HOUSE PUBLISHERS
Philadelphia

Frontispiece: Few occurrences could have been more destructive to a crowded, timber-built London of the 17th century than disease and fire. Both disasters struck in the 1660s with devastating and long-lasting results.

CHELSEA HOUSE PUBLISHERS

Editor in Chief Sally Cheney
Director of Production Kim Shinners
Production Manager Pamela Loos
Art Director Sara Davis
Production Editor Diann Grasse

Staff for THE GREAT PLAGUE AND FIRE OF LONDON

Editor LeeAnne Gelletly
Picture Research and Layout 21st Century Publishing
    and Communications, Inc.

First Printing

1 3 5 7 9 8 6 4 2

The Chelsea House World Wide Web address is
http://www.chelseahouse.com

Library of Congress Cataloging-in-Publication Data

Shields, Charles J., 1951–
    The Great Plague and Fire of London / Charles J. Shields
        p. cm—(Great disasters, reforms, and ramifications)
    Includes bibliographical references (p.   ) and index.
    Summary: A detailed history of two disasters that befell London, England: The Great Plague of 1665 in which it is estimated that at least 70,000 died, and the Great Fire of 1666, which destroyed four-fifths of the city.
    ISBN 0-7910-6324-0 (alk. paper)
    1. London (England)—History—17th century—Juvenile literature. 2. Plague—England—London—History—17th century—Juvenile literature. 3. Great Fire, London, England, 1666—Juvenile literature. [1. London (England)—History—17th century. 2. Plague—England—London. 3. Fires—England—London.] I. Title. II. Series.

DA681.S46 2001
942.1'2—dc21   2001042209

Contents

GREAT DISASTERS
REFORMS and RAMIFICATIONS

Jill McCaffrey
National Chairman
Armed Forces Emergency Services
American Red Cross

Introduction

Disasters have always been a source of fascination and awe. Tales of a great flood that nearly wipes out all life are among humanity's oldest recorded stories, dating at least from the second millennium B.C., and they appear in cultures from the Middle East to the Arctic Circle to the southernmost tip of South America and the islands of Polynesia. Typically gods are at the center of these ancient disaster tales—which is perhaps not too surprising, given the fact that the tales originated during a time when human beings were at the mercy of natural forces they did not understand.

To a great extent, we still are at the mercy of nature, as anyone who reads the newspapers or watches nightly news broadcasts can attest.

Hurricanes, earthquakes, tornados, wildfires, and floods continue to exact a heavy toll in suffering and death, despite our considerable knowledge of the workings of the physical world. If science has offered only limited protection from the consequences of natural disasters, it has in no way diminished our fascination with them. Perhaps that's because the scale and power of natural disasters force us as individuals to confront our relatively insignificant place in the physical world and remind us of the fragility and transience of our lives. Perhaps it's because we can imagine ourselves in the midst of dire circumstances and wonder how we would respond. Perhaps it's because disasters seem to bring out the best and worst instincts of humanity: altruism and selfishness, courage and cowardice, generosity and greed.

As one of the national chairmen of the American Red Cross, a humanitarian organization that provides relief for victims of disasters, I have had the privilege of seeing some of humanity's best instincts. I have witnessed communities pulling together in the face of trauma; I have seen thousands of people answer the call to help total strangers in their time of need.

Of course, helping victims after a tragedy is not the only way, or even the best way, to deal with disaster. In many cases planning and preparation can minimize damage and loss of life—or even avoid a disaster entirely. For, as history repeatedly shows, many disasters are caused not by nature but by human folly, shortsightedness, and unethical conduct. For example, when a land developer wanted to create a lake for his exclusive resort club in Pennsylvania's Allegheny Mountains in 1880, he ignored expert warnings and cut corners in reconstructing an earthen dam. On May 31, 1889, the dam gave way, unleashing 20 million tons of water on the towns below. The Johnstown Flood, the deadliest in American history, claimed more than 2,200 lives. Greed and negligence would figure prominently in the Triangle Shirtwaist Company fire in 1911. Deplorable conditions in the garment sweatshop, along with a failure to give any thought to the safety of workers, led to the tragic deaths of 146 persons. Technology outstripped wisdom only a year later, when the designers of the luxury liner *Titanic* smugly declared their state-of-the-art ship "unsinkable," seeing no need to provide lifeboat capacity for everyone onboard. On the night of April 14, 1912, more than 1,500 passengers and crew paid for this hubris with their lives after the ship collided with an iceberg and sank. But human catastrophes aren't always the unforeseen consequences of carelessness or folly. In the 1940s the leaders of Nazi Germany purposefully and systematically set out to exterminate all Jews, along with Gypsies, homosexuals, the mentally ill, and other so-called undesirables. More recently terrorists have targeted random members of society, blowing up airplanes and buildings in an effort to advance their political agendas.

The books in the GREAT DISASTERS: REFORMS AND RAMIFICA-TIONS series examine these and other famous disasters, natural and human made. They explain the causes of the disasters, describe in detail how events unfolded, and paint vivid portraits of the people caught up in dangerous circumstances. But these books are more than just accounts of what happened to whom and why. For they place the disasters in historical perspective, showing how people's attitudes and actions changed and detailing the steps society took in the wake of each calamity. And in the end, the most important lesson we can learn from any disaster—as well as the most fitting tribute to those who suffered and died—is how to avoid a repeat in the future.

Ring, a-Ring
a-Roses

Black Death, or bubonic plague, wiped out one-third of Europe's population in 1350. The disease is characterized by bruising and red rings that form around swellings near a person's ears, neck, armpits, or groin.

"I have heard that there might living creatures be seen by microscope, of strange, monstrous, and frightful shapes, such as dragons, serpents, and devils, horrible to behold. But this I very much questioned the truth of."

—Daniel Defoe, *Journal of the Plague Year*

In mid-December 1664, a hard frost fell on the city of London, usually a good sign that the weather would keep down the spread of disease. Then during the Christmas holidays, Dr. Nathaniel Hodges examined a young man with a high fever. Hodges treated him with "alexiterial" medicines—mainly potions that the doctor mixed himself.

But two days later, a pair of swellings the size of walnuts appeared on the inside of the patient's thighs—"buboes," non-medical people called them, a corruption of the Latin word *bubon,* or groin. Around both was a ring of bruising. Noting the swellings, their color, and other symptoms, Hodges decided there was no mistaking this "malignity," as he termed it. The young man had bubonic plague. Yet in spite of it, "by God's blessing the patient recovered," Hodges recalled years later in his 1672 book, *Loimologia: Or, an Historical Account of the Plague in London in 1665: With Precautionary Directions against the Like Contagion. (Loimologia* is a Greek word that might be translated as "plague-ology.")

Plague was by no means unknown in England, or anywhere else in all of Europe or the Near East. In 1350, 25 million people—one-third of Europe's population— died from it. Known as the Black Death in the 14th century because of its victims' telltale bruising, the disease caused swelling in lymph glands behind the ears, under the arms, on the neck, or in the groin. Tiny blood vessels broke and discolored the skin in splotchy reddish or black rings. Unknown to physicians of the day, the disease also infected the liver, spleen, and bone marrow.

It also deserved the name "Black Death" for another reason—because of the agony it caused its victims. The onset of plague brought chills, nausea, and vomiting. Then came feelings of anxiousness and sometimes delirium. Patients were known to fight off attempts to restrain them as they ran shrieking from their sick beds. The appearance of the dark, raised spots called "tokens" or "God's marks" meant the end was near, especially if the spots fused into carbuncles, large pus-filled boils, or sores. How long the disease would torment its victims varied—from a few hours to a few days, leaving the living to wonder at the mystery of this gruesome contagion. Often next of kin did not have long to mourn their loss. Plague was notorious for picking off whole families, one member at a time.

Although 17th-century Londoners were familiar with the plague's symptoms, they had no idea what caused it. One pattern they noted, however, was that it went hand in hand with filthiness. London was an ancient human habitation, dating from the days when the Roman army had built its outside walls. Without the means to provide sanitation for all its inhabitants, the city evolved into a breeding ground for epidemics.

London's "square mile" as it was called—really more of an oblong box with gates spaced regularly in the walls—backed up to the River Thames. Over the centuries, the city's location had guaranteed its prosperity. Ships and barges stocked with goods plied the river constantly. The overland trade entered London via the bridges that spanned the river, or through the city's gates, such as Ludgate, Aldersgate, Cripplegate, and Moorgate, for instance.

Steady commerce drew tradespeople. Probably for convenience, they grouped themselves into neighborhoods. The butchers preferred to do business in Newgate Street, where they slaughtered animals and hung the meat for sale in open stalls. The fish sellers hawked their wares in Billingsgate Market near the river. Candle makers worked near the river, too, on Thames Street, where the stench from their vats of boiling fat mingled with odors from nearby soap-boilers, dyers, and breweries. Worse still, in terms of smells, were the tanneries on the slope outside the city walls between Ludgate and Newgate. There, tanners created leather by soaking animal hides in a mixture of substances. One key ingredient was dog excrement.

But Londoners accepted stench as a natural hazard of living together. Householders dumped human waste into the street until the rain could wash it away. Deep ditches around the city walls were supposed to carry off some of the city's filth with the tide, but debris often blocked the flow. The open sewer of Houndsditch, for instance, got its name from the number of dead dogs floating in it.

As London's population increased, the city center became a maze of twisting, narrow streets, and its courtyards and alleys had nicknames that often became permanent—Three Legg Alley, Cock and Key Alley, Shoe Lane, Threadneedle Street, Mincing Lane, Bread Street, and Turnagain Lane (a dead end). Many streets were sunless because the roofs of the two-storied wooden buildings almost met overhead. Visitors, to get their bearings, looked for Old St. Paul's Cathedral, which dated from the 12th century. Easily visible, the cathedral's tower poked skyward, and its acres of rooftops covered with age-whitened lead reflected the sun.

To foreigners, however, London did not seem like an exceptionally dirty city. Other than being "densely crowded," as an ambassador from Venice reported to his superiors in 1618, it must have been one of the pleasanter cities of its day. The ambassador wrote, "The City of London renders itself truly worthy to be styled the metropolis of the kingdom, and the abode of royalty. . . . Two thirds of its extent consists in the suburbs where the nobility and the people also reside and where all the royal palaces, parks and gardens are situated. . . . The streets are commodious and wide with their shops furnished in every direction." The ambassador especially liked London Bridge lined with "houses and shops, so that it has rather the air of a long suburb than a handsome structure such as a bridge." About the same time, a member of a royal household visiting from Europe wrote that "Palaces are very common" in London, and attractive brick homes lined some streets.

But by then, the population of the packed city center was spilling over the old Roman walls into the suburbs, or

"Liberties" as they were called. A Royal Proclamation in 1580 warned that overcrowding invited plague:

> [W]here there are such great multitudes of people brought to inhabit in small rooms, whereof a great part are seen very poor, yea, such as must live by begging, or by worse means, and they heaped up together, and in a sort smothered with many families of children and servants in one house or small tenement; it must needs follow, if any plague or popular sickness should, by God's permission, enter among these multitudes, that the same would not only spread itself and invade the whole city and confines, but that a great mortality would ensue.

London had never been wholly free of plague, not for generations. The people dreaded outbreaks but regarded

The London of the 1650s was a bustling metropolis. It was home to the king, his court and government, universities, trade and commerce, an emerging middle class, and an exploding lower class—all squeezed into a few square miles.

Sanitation in London at this time was not ignored, but it wasn't carefully maintained either. Common practice allowed street gutters to fill with waste and trash, piles of refuse to accumulate at the ends of streets, and open ditches and sewers around the outside of the city walls to remain only partially drained.

them as natural, too. All through the Middle Ages and most of the 17th century, plague festered and erupted, mainly in poor areas where living conditions were the worst.

London authorities did not just wait for disaster to happen. There were standing laws, although not very well enforced, about sanitation. Citizen watchdogs were appointed by the city to "inquire about people, who after rain, throw dung, rubbish, sea-coal ashes, rushes, or any other nuisance into the Thames or channels of the City." Moreover, all householders were required to keep the streets clean in front of their homes. Dutifully, the people shoved garbage that the rain had not washed from the kennels, or gutters, into piles at the end of the streets where city rakers were supposed to collect it—waste from butcher shops, food scraps, and the carcasses of animals, such as wild cats and dogs. These reeking heaps, however, attracted and nourished the real carriers of plague— flea-infested black rats.

Not even the most educated person at that time would have guessed that fleas were responsible for spreading plague. Fleas were as ordinary as ants and everyone itched and scratched from them. The places where the poor crowded together to do their shopping in the seedier parts of the city were jokingly called "flea markets." With insect bodies no bigger than poppy seeds, how could fleas contain organisms invisible to the eye? Writer Daniel Defoe, who survived the Great Plague of 1665 as a child and would later pen the famous novel *Robinson Crusoe,* scoffed at the idea of invisible creatures. "I have heard that there might living creatures be seen by microscope," he wrote in his 1722 book *Journal of the Plague Year*, "of strange, monstrous, and frightful shapes, such as dragons, serpents, and devils, horrible to behold. But this I very much questioned the truth of."

There was no lack of theories about how plague spread, even among the educated. Dr. Hodges, who examined the feverish young man in December 1664, blamed the spread of plague on "poisonous steams." Dr. William Boghurst, another London physician living at the same time as Hodges, argued that plague became an epidemic when it was helped by "standing and stinking waters; dung hills, excrements, dead bodies lying unburied and putrefying; churchyards too full crammed;

unseasonable weather." Like Hodges, Boghurst also published an account of the plague. His 1666 book was entitled *Loimographia: An Account of the Great Plague of London in the Year 1665.* It was obvious to doctors and scientists of the day that plague and unhealthy situations were connected somehow. But without an understanding of the unseen world of bacteria, everyone was baffled by the step-by-step spread of the disease.

Actually, the way plague spread was simple. For a full-blown epidemic to occur, the conditions affecting fleas, rats, and weather had to be in perfect balance. Black rats can be carriers of the deadly plague bacterium, *Yersinia pestis.* In a city like London, which offered the cool, shady alleys, cellars, and warehouses the rats preferred, the population of infected rats rose and fell in response to the environment. The numbers increased when the rat population bred rapidly enough to replace rats sick and dying from plague, or when a fresh population of infected rats arrived in ships, for instance. Rats, like most warm-blooded wild animals, have fleas, which live by biting and drawing blood. When an infected rat died, its fleas leaped to a new host (fleas can jump nearly six feet). If a flea carrying the plague bacterium bit a rat not infected with plague, that rat died in about five days. If an infected flea bit a human being, that person died in eight to eleven days. In the right circumstances—a large population of rats, some of them infected, and warm, dry weather that sped up flea-hatching—an outbreak of bubonic plague was likely.

Three times already during the 17th century, the ideal conditions for catastrophe had arisen. In 1603, an outbreak of plague killed 37,294 Londoners; in 1625, a second epidemic killed 35,417; and in 1636, another 10,400 died.

In fact, Londoners expected plague to reappear about

every 20 years. And as the spring of 1665 arrived, many predicted that a fresh outbreak was long overdue. Word had reached the city that tens of thousands had died from plague in Holland in 1663. Children chanted a rhyme about rings of reddish plague spots and how people carried sweet-smelling flowers in their pockets to keep away the disease. The rhyme, a form of which is still chanted on playgrounds today, went:

> Ring a-ring a-Roses
> A pocketful of posies
> 'Tishoo, 'tishoo,
> We all fall down!

Within less than a year, more than 1 in 7 people in the city of London—over 68,000—would "fall down" and die of bubonic plague.

Fleas infected with the plague jumped from rats to other animals and to people. In the 17th century, over 151,000 Londoners died of the disease. Some tried to flee the city during the plague of 1630, as depicted in the drawing above, only to find they were not welcome elsewhere. Any stranger was considered a potential carrier of pestilence.

The name of this alley in London in the 1600s, Gin Lane, hints at the crowded and lawless conditions of the city's back streets. Impoverished people, servants, and criminals mingled together while purchasing provisions, seeking diversion, and begging for charity. The civil and religious rule of the Lord Mayor of London and the Church of England had little control here.

The Outbreak

"[The plague] suddenly got strength, and spread abroad its fatal poisons; and merely for want of confining the persons first seized with it, the whole city was in a little time irrecoverably infected."

—Dr. Nathaniel Hodges, 1672

On the eve of the Great Plague in the spring of 1665, 460,000 people lived in noisy, congested London. As the sun rose each day, the air was often foggy with an "impure and thick mist," complained a Londoner, from coal fires used for heating. Near Chancery Court, the proprietors of taverns, eating houses, inns, and coffeehouses prepared for the arrival of early customers connected with the legal profession—secretaries, bailiffs, and lawyers and their clients. Along upscale Fleet Street, merchants opened their doors for business—the woolen-drapers, grocers, saddle-makers, upholsterers, fruiterers, tobacconists, gunsmiths, booksellers, and gold- and silver-smiths. Behind main thoroughfares like Fleet Street was "a labyrinth of alleys and yards," wrote historian Justin Champion in a paper analyzing epidemics in London. In that labyrinth, servants, porters, and laundry maids sent on errands bumped elbows with housewives, soldiers, beggars, tradespeople, apprentices, and prostitutes.

In the narrow streets and alleys, people jostled each other as they tried to "keep to the wall" on either side, away from the mud and garbage down the middle of the passages. There was no tradition of keeping to the left or the right—everyone shouldered his way past people coming in the other direction. Wagons and coaches paid no heed to anyone, forcing pedestrians to get out of the way or risk being trampled. Conversation was carried on at a half-shout over the constant din. Hawkers with baskets of fish calling "Mackerel! Fresh mackerel!" competed with milkmaids' cries of "Milk below!" to windows overhead. Polite society avoided these neighborhoods because, as Champion wrote, "back streets like Ram and Whites Alley, or Whitefriars, were infamous for being overcrowded with 'disabled and loose kinds of lodgers,' and with lewd houses, debtors, vagabonds and 'unbridled lawlessness.'"

London combated this lawlessness by relying mainly on the same two authorities that governed the rest of England. One was secular, or nonreligious. That was the king, Charles II, the king's advisors such as the Privy Council, the Parliament, and a host of appointed or elected officials including the Lord Mayor of London. A second form of government looked after the spiritual side of English Christians—the Anglican Church, or Church of England.

Under this dual system for maintaining law and order, London in 1665 consisted of 26 political wards and an astounding 109 church-run parishes inside the old Roman walls. A parish provided people living within its boundaries with spiritual and legal benefits—church services, baptisms, marriages and, at the end of life, sanctified burials. Churches were so abundant inside London's square mile that congregations could hear each other singing on Sunday mornings.

This particular dual system of authority had only recently been restored after more than a decade-long interruption. For many years, religion had been the cause of bloodshed in England, Ireland, Scotland, and Wales. The Protestant Reformation of the mid-1500s, born of an attempt to reform the Catholic church, ignited outright civil war between Catholics and Protestants until Elizabeth I sought to unite the two factions under the Church of England during her reign. By borrowing practices and beliefs from both the Catholic and Protestant religions, the Church of England created a mistrustful truce for a time.

But then during the reign of Charles I, Puritan leader and Parliament member Oliver Cromwell raised an army bent on reforming England's political, social, and religious life by force. Charles I was arrested by Puritans and beheaded in 1649, after which a semi-democratic government called the Commonwealth replaced the monarchy. The morally conservative Puritan regime destroyed or closed places of public entertainment, such as the Globe Theater, formerly owned by William Shakespeare and company. Cromwell, appointed Lord Protector of the Commonwealth, persecuted his political and religious enemies in order to consolidate his power. Catholics in Ireland suffered especially hard.

King Charles I was executed on January 30, 1649, by opposition leader Oliver Cromwell, who sought to forcefully change England's political, social, and religious life. This rebellion resulted in a semi-democratic Commonwealth and lasted nine years until his death in 1658.

The revolution turned out to be short-lived. After Cromwell's death in 1658, support for the Commonwealth evaporated. In 1660, Charles II—the son of the deposed king—returned to the throne by popular acclaim. The new king was witty, outgoing, well educated, and broad-minded. Charles II's reign—later known as the Restoration because the monarchy was restored—had so far been a merry one. Actually, some thought it too merry. The London theaters reopened and received royal encouragement from the king himself. A rush of bold new plays poked fun at everything serious. Riotous entertainment became popular among the well-to-do, and fashion imitated French extravagance. The wealthy favored gorgeous silk clothes and elaborate wigs. Men wore hose stockings, women displayed their breasts in low-cut bodices, and pretty manners—bowing and curtseying—became the rage. The rich nestled into newly built residential squares in elite neighborhoods such as St. James, Mayfair, and Marylebone.

The Restoration did not improve or change life for most people in London, however, or in the rest of England for that matter. Most Londoners were far outside the halls of power and influence, especially if they were poor, Jews, foreigners, Catholics (who were forbidden to worship in public), those who sympathized with the now-defeated Puritan cause, or among those Protestants who refused to join the Church of England. This splinter group of Protestants, known as Nonconformists, included Methodists, Quakers, Presbyterians, and Congregationalists. Under Charles II's Act of Uniformity in 1662, some Protestant ministers lost their positions because they refused to be, or could not be because of their beliefs, ordained as ministers by the Church of England.

So many upheavals of church and state coming one right after another—bloodshed over religion, the execution of a king, and the antics of the aristocracy—convinced more than a few Londoners that a reckoning, or punishment, was due.

Clergyman Thomas Reeves distributed a pamphlet in 1657 warning that God's answer to sinful behavior would be plague. "What inventions shall you then be put to," he asked scornfully, "when your sins shall have shut up all the conduits of the city, when you shall see no men of your incorporation, but the mangled citizen; nor hear no noise in your streets but the cries, the shrieks, the yells and pangs of gasping, dying men; when among the throngs of associates not a man will own you or come near you?"

Doomsayers like Reeves were not regarded as cranks, either. The English put great stock in supernatural signs and fortune-telling. London physician William Boghurst, who had several theories on the causes of a plague epidemic, also dabbled in pointing out the signs foretelling such an epidemic. In *Loimographia,* he listed "signs foreshowing a plague coming," which included "comets, gleams of fire and fiery impressions in the air," children acting out funerals,

After Cromwell's death, King Charles II landed at Dover to take back power and restore the monarchy to its former glory. The luxurious extravagance of Charles's court during this period caused many English to worry that God would punish their kingdom for its wayward government.

women miscarrying, fruit turning bad without explanation, and "ill conditions of the stars, if you will believe in astrologers." Many people did believe in the forecasts of astrologers. In fact, a picture of one astrologer in particular, William Lilly, could be seen hanging inside homes as often as memorial ones of the assassinated king, Charles I.

In 1665 London, Lilly, in his early sixties, was quite famous and an adviser to powerful people. His position of influence was unusual for the son of a yeoman—or middle-class—farmer, because it was very difficult to change social classes in 17th-century England. In grammar school, Lilly learned Latin from an exceptionally fine teacher—he would later write all his astrology books in Latin. At 17, he went to work as a servant for a wealthy Londoner, marrying his employer's widow eight years later. Then six years after that, she too died, and Lilly inherited all the property. At the age of 30, he began studying astrology seriously.

His first almanac of astrology, printed in 1644, was a great success and was translated into several languages. His books of astrological signs and explanations continued to appear over the years, full of mysterious remarks. Although he claimed "I do no new thing, I do herein but imitate the Ancients [Egyptians]," he enjoyed being nicknamed the English Merlin, after the wizard of King Arthur's court. Years after the Great Plague of 1665, Lilly took credit for predicting it as early as 1651 in his book *Monarchy or No Monarchy*. "[W]herein you may see the representation of people in their winding sheets, persons digging graves and sepulchres, coffins, etc. All this was performed by the more Secret Key of Astrology," he boasted.

The weather turned warm again in London in March 1665. Then in early April, a spectacular heavenly event astonished everyone—a comet streaked over London, an occurrence traditionally believed to warn of a great happening—usually a disastrous one. Astrologers like Lilly seized the moment to draw attention to themselves by making sensational predictions. Dr. Hodges wrote disgustedly about the "star-gazers" that fed people's fears and put them in a weakened state of mind. "The people therefore were frightened without reason at such things, and the mischief was much more in the predictions of the star-gazers, than in the stars themselves: nothing could however conquer these sad impressions, so powerful were they among the populace, who anticipated their unhappy fate with their fears."

But even Hodges himself noted that two or three members of the same family in the parish of Westminster had died of plague at the end of 1664. In addition, news of the terrible plague epidemic in Holland in 1663, which had probably originated in Turkey in 1661, persuaded the king's Privy Council to quarantine all vessels arriving from ports where the disease had been reported.

For a time, the quarantining of ships seemed to be working, at least according to figures in the Bills of Mortality. Ever since the devastating outbreak of plague in 1603, the monthly Bill of Mortality reported deaths in every parish and their cause. As of early 1665, the Bills of Mortality showed no increase in the number of plague deaths, which was a good sign. Only three deaths from plague—a little higher than usual—were recorded in April.

However, near the end of April, a sinister pattern began to emerge, one feared by everyone old enough to remember the outbreak of 1636. Suddenly, more cases of plague were being reported. By the end of May, the number of plague deaths in the poor parish of St. Giles-in-the-Fields had jumped abruptly to 43. That was how plague epidemics had always started in London—they erupted among the impoverished as the weather grew warmer, and then, like summer storms gathering strength, they burst down upon the general populace. Dr. Hodges said the effect of the increase in plague victims was electric: "everyone predicted [the plague's] future

The epidemic, produced by conditions including a hot, dry summer, also came during a stressful time of war with Holland. Earlier onslaughts of the disease had determined common plague practices and customs, such as quickly and unceremoniously burying the dead.

devastations, and they terrified each other with remembrances of a former pestilence."

From the government's point of view, the timing of the outbreak couldn't be worse. In March, England had waded into a war with Holland over trade, and plague would be interpreted by the Dutch enemy as weakness. Moreover, English merchant ships might be quarantined in foreign ports, injuring overseas trade. London journalist and newspaper publisher Roger L'Estrange tried to calm people's fears by printing in his *Intelligencer* that reports of plague were exaggerated.

What no one could ignore, however, were the words, "God Have Mercy on this House" and a red cross appearing on more and more front doors. By law, when plague was detected in a London house, all the inhabitants, the sick and the well, were shut up inside together for 40 days to contain the disease. The words of prayer and the red cross served as an official warning that plague was within the house.

Watchmen, called warders, placed food and water on the doorstep, or passed it through the window, spending most of their time making sure no one entered or left. Then at the end of 40 days, a white cross replaced the red one, and the quarantine continued for another 20 days, after which the house was supposed to be fumigated with burning sulfur and its walls sprinkled with powdery lime.

During times when some kind of harm seemed near, Londoners purchased special charms with superstitious powers to protect themselves. During the spring of 1665, as the plague gained strength, peddlers did a brisk business selling wax images of saints, lucky bracelets, little twists of paper containing powder of dried toads, walnuts filled with mercury worn around the neck, rings displaying a skull and crossbones, and patches dipped in arsenic. One item, a printed spell, was an old favorite and sold well. It read:

ABRACADABRA
ABRACADABR
ABRACADAB
ABRACADA
ABRACAD
ABRACA
ABRAC
ABRA
ABR
AB
A

On April 30, Samuel Pepys (pronounced "peeps"), a Royal Navy administrator, wrote in his diary of the growing sense of alarm in London as word of quarantined households spread. "Great fears of the sickness here in the city, it being said that two or three houses are already shut up. God preserve us all!"

In the summer of 1665, throngs of people escaped the infected city of London. First the nobility left, then the upper, middle, and lower classes, and finally even the very symbol of England: the king and his court. Many ministers and doctors, professionals most needed by the afflicted, deserted the city despite pleas to stay.

Exodus from London

"I find all the town almost going out of town, the coaches and wagons being all full of people going into the country."

—Samuel Pepys, June 21, 1665

On June 5, 1665, the Lord Chamberlain ordered the theaters closed. The number of cases of plague was clearly on the rise. By early June, the roads leading out of London were already clogged with people fleeing the city in carriages, on horseback, and on foot. Dr. Hodges said "all doors and passages are thronged for escape" as if people were running from a fire. The nobility were the first to leave because they had the money to easily afford a temporary move, followed by the merchants

Former government clerk, Samuel Pepys (1633–1703), was promoted to a high-paying job in the naval office. He had to stay in London during the plague, therefore, and noted many observations of the event in his secret diary. His account is gossipy but is still a vital, eyewitness report.

and the lawyers. From the doorway of the Cross Keys tavern near Cripplegate, one of his favorite places to have a mug of ale, Samuel Pepys, the naval administrator, watched the migration take place.

We know about Pepys's movements almost day by day because of a secret diary he kept, beginning on January 1, 1660. He was then a 26-year-old clerk for the government, "very poor," he confided to his diary, and married to Elizabeth, an attractive but rather flighty young woman, who was seven years younger. Perhaps Pepys sensed that his fortunes were about to change when he started his diary, because they did almost overnight. Charles II was restored to the throne in May 1660, and government posts were reassigned to families who had remained loyal to the king during Cromwell's Puritan rule. By a stroke of luck, an influential relative of Pepys's, the Earl of Sandwich, obtained for him an important spot in the navy office. Pepys's job was to keep the fleet supplied with provisions and equipment, such as sails, rigging, food, armament, and so on. The change in his career instantly lifted him out of shabbiness and into the ranks of the upper middle class. In July 1660, he and Elizabeth moved into a house on Seething Lane, next door to the navy office, that was specially provided for them.

During the next nine and a half years, Pepys wrote in his diary several nights a week. (His favorite way to conclude an entry was "And so to bed.") But he disguised everything he wrote with an ingenious and complicated code, which was not deciphered until a century after his death. Like most diarists, he did not want anyone to read his private thoughts. He confided on paper things he did not want Elizabeth to know about—his thoughts about other women, his feelings about her, and even his unfaithfulness at times. Yet he is also an excellent observer of himself, providing a frank and interesting portrait of his life and what it was like to be living in London during the mid-17th century.

Pepys was vain and he realized it, unable to resist strolling around outside during the plague just "to show, forsooth, my new suit" of black silk. He was excited by science and purchased a telescope when astronomy in Europe was still a young field. He was a prolific reader, and he proudly noted the progress being made on a new bookcase he had commissioned to hold his collection of 3,000 volumes. He was welcome in the royal household and knew the king and his ministers personally, although he was unimpressed by royalty, for some reason. Pepys also laughed at his own self-importance on occasion, too. With a dry sense of humor, he described an episode in which he made a fool of himself at a party by accidentally setting his wig on fire. "[It] made such an odd noise, nobody could tell what it was till they saw the flame, my back being to the candle!" As an eyewitness to the historic events in London in 1665 and 1666, we could have no better reporter on the ground than Pepys.

However, by a wonderful coincidence, there was another excellent diarist writing at that time: John Evelyn, a friend of Pepys's. It's not clear whether the two men knew they were both keeping diaries—it was a common hobby among educated people—but taken together their accounts of London provide an even richer perspective. Pepys was a keen—and gossipy—observer of people and their behavior. He relished a good story. Evelyn, on the other hand, noted the facts of what he saw, usually without passing judgment. But facts by themselves can be powerfully descriptive too, as when Evelyn described walking through the burned-out neighborhoods after the Great Fire of 1666: "The ground under my feet was so hot, that it even burnt the soles of my shoes."

Evelyn kept his diary for an astounding 66 years until his death in 1706. Thirteen years older than Pepys, Evelyn met the younger man through their work for the king. Evelyn was commissioner for prisoners of war and for sick and wounded seamen, which would have brought him to the navy office regularly even though his house, Sayes Court, was in Deptford, a town outside of London. Unlike Pepys,

Another government employee, John Evelyn, also kept a diary during the plague years. More educated and wealthier than Pepys, the two were business associates and friends. Evelyn wrote from his estate outside of London but was frequently in town; he toured burned-out neighborhoods right after the Great Fire of London in 1666.

Evelyn was independently wealthy—his grandfather had introduced the manufacture of gunpowder to England—so his work for the government was done more out of a sense of loyalty than out of necessity. Evelyn's real passions were his hobbies—gardening (his private gardens were famous, and he may have invented the first heated greenhouse) and the humanities—art, literature, and science. Pepys admired Evelyn and probably regarded him as a role model, although he privately confessed to his diary that his friend sometimes acted a little conceited, especially when he insisted on reading his poetry aloud while Pepys listened, bored and annoyed.

In Pepys's entries for June 1665, he begins mentioning plague more and more often, reflecting the rising anxiety among his fellow Londoners. On June 7, for example, he recorded, "This day, much against my will, I did in Drury Lane see two or three houses with a red cross upon the doors, and 'Lord have mercy upon us,' writ there; which was a sad sight to me, being the first of the kind that, to my remembrance I ever saw." The sight made him cautious, and he purchased some tobacco "to smell to and chaw." Raw tobacco, it was believed, somehow helped counteract plague. Pepys also carried a lucky rabbit's foot, a charm that could still be seen hanging from key chains and rearview mirrors as recently as 30 years ago.

Ten days later, a second incident occurred that left him shaken, as though the plague had made a pass at him and missed. On June 17, he took a hackney coach—the equivalent of a taxicab—from the Lord Treasurer's house, located on the outskirts of St. Giles-in-the-Fields. St. Giles was one of the poor parishes outside the city walls where plague cases had first been reported. As the coach made its way along Holborne Street, Pepys noticed they were going slower and slower. Finally, the coachman got down from his seat "hardly able to stand," Pepys said, "and told me that he was suddenly struck very sick, and almost blind, he could not see." Pepys got out and found another hackney to take, feeling sorry to abandon the poor man in the street, but implying by his actions that he was looking after his own safety, too. He ended the entry, "God have mercy upon us all."

By mid-June, the crush of people trying to leave London raised the question of whether city officials had

the situation under control. So far, the outbreak was mainly in the poor parishes outside the walls. An epidemic inside the old city would only make the exodus worse. The Lord Mayor responded by closing the city's gates to anyone outside the walls not having an official certificate of health from a physician. Business boomed for apothecaries, or druggists, and physicians alike. Dr. Boghurst, practicing in St. Giles, reported seeing 50 to 60 people a day, both the well and the sick.

The demand for health certificates could not keep up with the supply, and forgers pocketed a tidy sum selling fake ones. On June 21, the Privy Council directed city officials to put warders in the streets and

There were several fronts in the battle against the 1665 plague. Patients needed to be fed and nursed, victims needed to be collected and buried, and guards had to stop people traveling from infected areas to noninfected areas, as depicted above, to prevent the spread of contagion.

passages leading to St. Giles, where the number of plague deaths had already topped 300 for the month. The warders were to stop any "loose persons" and anyone suspected of coming from infected households. The order came too late, however. The plague had already entered the city center of London. Parishes inside the city walls were reporting an increase in the number of burials due to death from plague.

By the third week of June, the king's advisors had persuaded him to leave with the royal household and relocate to Hampton Court, about 20 miles down the Thames River from London, until at least the winter. Most of the gentry, or well-to-do, had already left, after all. No one was surprised when Charles II, in the best interests of the nation, departed in a royal procession out of the city gates. But many were shocked by the number of doctors and ministers who trailed in the king's wake.

The doctors who fled made the excuse that they could do more good by surviving the outbreak. But the ministers who left apparently slipped away without explanation. The bishop of London warned them that they would be replaced, privately worrying that Nonconformist Protestant ministers would seize the opportunity to preach in their vacant pulpits. But the bishop's threat made few of the runaway ministers turn around. Among angry and disappointed churchgoers, a bitter pamphlet gained wide readership. Its title was *A Pulpit for Let* (for rent).

Thomas Vincent, a Nonconformist minister who had lost his own London pulpit under the Act of Uniformity, spoke for many who felt abandoned in his 1667 pamphlet, *God's Terrible Voice in the City.* "I do not blame many citizens retiring, when there was so little trading, and the presence of all might have helped forward the increase and spreading of the infection; but how did guilt drive many away, where duty would have engaged them to stay in the place?" Likewise, Dr. Boghurst was shocked that professionals could so easily ignore their conscience in times of crisis. "Every man that undertakes to be of a profession or takes upon him any office must take all parts of it," he wrote, "the good and the evil, the pleasure and the pain, the profit and the inconvenience altogether, and not pick and choose; for ministers must preach, captains must fight, physicians attend upon the sick, etc." Vincent and Boghurst stayed behind, Vincent finding an empty pulpit to preach from—as the Bishop of London feared would happen—and Boghurst continuing to treat the sick in the badly stricken parish of St. Giles.

Pepys had no choice but to stay. His duties in the navy office were important because England was at war with Holland. In his diary, he never expresses a wish to go. However, he did make sure that his family left for safety.

On June 22, he made arrangements for his mother to go into the country. She annoyed her son when she spent too much time trying to make up her mind whether to go and what to take and "lost her place in the coach" Pepys had arranged. She had to sit in an open wagon instead. Two weeks later, on July 5, Pepys saw Elizabeth and her two maids off to Woolwich, a country town, assuring himself "very prettily accommodated they will be." The parting was sad. He noted, "I left them going to supper, grieved in my heart to part with my wife, being worse by much without her, though some trouble there is in having the care of a family at home in this plague time." Aware of the danger he was in, he put all of his affairs in order, including redrafting his will, conscious that "a man cannot depend on living two days to an end."

Meanwhile, at Sayes Court in Deptford, Pepys's fellow diarist John Evelyn noted on June 28 that meetings of his favorite organization, the Royal Society, an elite group devoted to the study of science, had been called off for the rest of the summer because of plague. He does not express any personal concern, though, suggesting that the disease was still limited to London.

Outside of London, however, most people were taking no chances. When fleeing Londoners arrived in the countryside, they were often shunned. Even letters received from the capital received cautious treatment; they were scraped, heated, soaked, aired, and pressed flat to eliminate "pestilential matter." Some city dwellers, anxious to evacuate, found that no towns would accept them, and they ended up camping out. In his *Journal of the Plague Year,* Daniel Defoe described the situation of watermen who normally made their livings by ferrying people in boats up and down the Thames. Having taken their families out of London by boat, they were marooned on the banks of the river, "their whole families in their boats, covered with tilts and bales, as they call them and furnished with straw within for their lodging, and that they lay thus all along by the shore in the marshes, some of them setting up little tents with their sails, and so lying under them on shore in the day, and going into their boats at night; and in this manner, I have heard, the river-sides were lined with boats and people as long as they had anything to subsist on, or could get anything of the country."

Someone who did make a successful exit to the countryside, however, was astrologer William Lilly. Some of the poor had been coming to him in London, bringing urine from infected victims. They would

stand respectfully at a distance, hoping he could perform some kind of magic with the substance. Instead, he told them the sick should drink cordials, or strong liquids, which would make them sweat, "whereby many recovered," he claimed. But his landlord did not want visits from persons who had been around plague. "My landlord of the house was afraid of those poor people, I nothing at all," Lilly wrote. "He was desirous I should be gone; he had four children, I took them with me into the country and provided for them." On June 27, he departed with his wife and family, with the landlord's four children in his care.

And then, Lilly noted with obvious satisfaction, "six weeks after I departed, he, his wife and many servants died of the Plague."

At first, city dwellers needed "clean bills of health" before they were given permission to travel. Soon, however, the country fell into a lawless state and people left London in a panic using any method available, including traveling by water in boats and barges.

"Bring Out Your Dead!"

The horror of seeing tens of thousands of corpses dulled the usual respect toward the deceased. Men with carts traveled through parishes to pick up bodies during the plague of 1664–5 and greeted everyone with the matter-of-fact cry, "Bring out your dead!"

"If any voice be heard, it is the groans of dying persons, breathing forth their last, and the funeral knells of them that are ready to be carried to their graves."

—Thomas Vincent, clergyman

Records from London parishes show that by the first week of July, the city was fighting the outbreak on several fronts. The most efficient way for officials to manage the epidemic was to work through the parishes. Most parishes were anchored by churches, each one administered by a small staff. The minister of the church looked after the spiritual needs of the parishioners; the churchwarden served as the secretary, treasurer, and record keeper of the building; and the sexton managed the affairs of the cemetery—scheduling burials and supervising the work of the grave diggers. The church's budget came under the control of a local board of church members. For coordinating efforts against an epidemic, parish churches provided a citywide network.

During times of plague, the parishes had emergency funds available through a 1603 statute—the year of a previous outbreak—granting church officials the power to raise money for support of the poor, "lest they should wander abroad and thereby infect others," the law read. The money could be put to four uses—paying relief to families unable to work; purchasing supplies and nursing services for the sick; paying watchmen's wages for keeping an eye on infected households; and paying for various services such as grave digging, placing locks on doors, or carrying away corpses.

By late June, for example, the parish of St. Dunstan's Vestry had appointed watchers—listed as Thomas Welham and Francis Cooper—who were assigned to survey the surrounding streets. They checked to see that quarantine measures were being carried out. If the proper procedures were being followed, the sick would be shut up inside the house together with the well with whom they had come in contact—in fact often whole families were quarantined together. The required and now too familiar red cross and "God Have Mercy on this House" would appear. Posted outside would be one or two warders to guard the house and pass in food, water, and medicine. As watchers, Welham and Cooper were also expected to monitor who passed through the neighborhood. Strangers in time of plague were suspicious.

Identifying new cases of plague so quarantine measures could be put in place was the job of searchers. St. Dunstan's hired two women for two shillings a week

Crosses marked on houses signaled to other citizens of the plague illness within. The 60-day quarantine forced both sick and ill to stay inside together, away from much-needed fresh air, exercise, and food. Most families did not survive the conditions.

as searchers—widows Briggs and Manton (we only know their last names). It was an unpleasant and even gruesome responsibility. According to instructions issued by the College of Physicians of London, they were to check for any "swellings, risings, or botch under the ear, about the neck, on either side, or under the armpits of either side, or the groins." Then they were to look for a "blister, much bigger than the small pox, of straw color or livid color . . . easily eating deep into the flesh, and sometimes having a black crust upon it." This was a "token" or "God's mark," as people called it. Positive identification of plague meant that the sick person could not be removed from the house, no matter where he or she was found, and that the house must be quarantined. However, parishes also had the option of opening "pest houses" to which plague-stricken persons could be taken and cared for along with dozens of other sufferers. As the disease progressed, pest houses sprang up all around the outskirts of the city.

From a medical man's point of view, Dr. Nathaniel Hodges doubted the wisdom of the quarantine measures. First, he noted that placing a red cross on the door caused neighbors to flee, "who otherwise might have been a help to [the sick] on many accounts." Secondly, the practice of keeping the sick and well shut up together, without access to fresh air and exercise, made little sense to him. "Liberty . . . is necessary for the comforts both of body and mind," he wrote. And third, he thought that the sick and the possibly infected well should be separated, the well to "proper accommodations out of the city" and the sick to "convenient apartments provided on purpose for them." That way, he argued, plague carriers could be isolated comfortably from everyone else.

His suggestions seem like common sense now. And perhaps if the city had had time to react to the outbreak, "proper accommodations" could have been planned. But without knowledge of how plague was spread, and with plague deaths in London beginning to soar by mid-July to more than 1,000 a week, city officials instead made a stab at a quick solution.

As a first step, the city government made it illegal to keep domestic pigs, dogs, cats, pigeons, and rabbits. Probably, if a family had pets, they let them go rather than be found in violation of the law. Then the Lord Mayor ordered workers into the streets to kill stray dogs and cats in the city. It had been done before in London during plagues. Everyone knew that filth was somehow

connected to contagion, and garbage-eating dogs in the streets and mangy cats appeared to be part of the problem. In short order, the dogcatcher for the parish of St. Margaret, Westminster, submitted a bill for producing 353 dead dogs. By the end of the summer, exterminators had killed a total of 40,000 dogs and 200,000 cats, estimated Defoe in *Journal of the Plague Year*. Stray pigs wandered the alleys, too, but they were valuable and were impounded or sold.

Now the rats, with their natural enemies the cats out of the way, flourished—and so did the plague. Parish records show how the shadow of the epidemic stretched across the city in July, touching everywhere. St. Bride's burial register records 32 burials in May, for instance,

The causes of the disease were unknown in the 17th century, but people believed the city's foul air and filth were primary factors of infection. Animals, such as dogs and cats, commonly ate garbage and other refuse. They were killed by the hundreds of thousands in an attempt to quell the plague.

then 22 in the first half of June and 34 in the second half. So many bodies arriving at the parish cemeteries presented a practical problem that strained the resources of the churches. All parishioners had the right to be buried in the church cemetery, but the number of dead kept rising.

At St. Bride's, the churchwarden directed the sexton not to accept any more bodies from the neighboring parish of St. Martin Ludgate, except on payment of double duties "because our ground begins to fill." On July 3, the parish decided to pay the grave digger extra to encourage him to dig graves as deep as required and as quickly as possible. As expenses mounted, parish officials were forced to cut corners, and they suspended the practice of supplying coffins for the elderly and children. According to its records, St. Bride's stopped purchasing coffins after July 26 in the middle of a two-week period when 110 bodies arrived for burial. Sheets and shrouds were used to wrap the dead instead.

Collecting the corpses soon became a critical task. The parishes of St. Bride's and St. Dunstan's purchased "slings to carry the dead corpses," and jointly hired bearers to retrieve the bodies. Other parishes, especially the large ones, bought or hired carts. These dead carts, as they were known, creaked along the streets and passages at night announced by regular cries of "Bring out your dead!" and the ringing of a bell. Grieving family members hailed the cart, then carried out the deceased. The bearers, who were usually smoking tobacco to prevent infection, wrestled the body onto the heap of others while grieving family members watched. Slowly, the cart continued on its way, eventually returning to the parish cemetery to unload its ghastly freight.

Once, at least, the dead-cart bearers were too conscientious in their duties. Defoe related the story he heard of a drunken street-musician collected for burial by John Hayward, under-sexton of St. Stephen's parish:

> As soon as the cart stopped the fellow awakened and struggled a little to get his head out from among the dead bodies, when, raising himself up in the cart, he called out, "Hey! Where am I?" This frighted the fellow that attended about the work; but after some pause John Hayward, recovering himself, said, "Lord bless us! There's somebody in the cart not quite dead!" So another called to him and said, "Who are you?" The fellow answered, "I am the poor piper. Where am I?" "Where are you?" says Hayward. "Why, you are in the dead cart, and we are going to bury you." "But I an't dead though, am I?" says the piper, which made them laugh a little, though, as John said, they were heartily frighted at first; so they helped the poor fellow down, and he went about his business.

Collecting the dead wasn't the only problem. Managing the sick was becoming increasingly difficult. In the poor parishes, the situation began to spin out of control. Shutting up a household in a better neighborhood could be accomplished step by step, but in alleys, passageways, and dead-end courtyards where homeless, beggars, and "loose persons" could be found, quarantine measures were nearly impossible. The sick broke into public places raving. "Some of the infected run about staggering like drunken men," wrote Dr. Hodges, "and fall and expire in the streets, while others lie half-dead and comatose . . . others fall dead in the market, while they are buying necessaries for the support of life." Clergyman Thomas Vincent described encountering a man who "through the dizziness of his head with the disease, which seized upon him there, had dashed his face against the wall; and when I came by, he lay hanging with his bloody face over the

An absence of hard medical knowledge fostered several types of folk medicine. Flowers, herbs, and tobacco were thought to ward off the "foul air" associated with the plague. Here, men smoke tobacco as they cart off the corpses in the attempt to avoid infection.

rails, and bleeding upon the ground." Vincent later found him lying in the shade of a tree and tried to speak to him, "but he could make me no answer, but rattled in the throat, and as I was informed, within half an hour died in the place."

Even in the streets where warders kept guard, the situation was hardly better. Vincent said he heard of "some in their frenzy, rising out of their beds, and leaping about their rooms; others crying and roaring at their windows; some coming forth almost naked, and running into the streets." Defoe claimed that a man driven frantic with pain and fear ran naked from his house and jumped into the Thames River. He swam to the opposite bank and back again. Climbing out of the water, he found that the cold of the water had lowered his fever and the exertion had broken the swellings. In a few days, he recovered.

The plague was not uniform in how it attacked, adding to its mystery. Drs. Hodges and Boghurst tried to recognize patterns, but they were often baffled. Hodges examined a girl who seemed so healthy that he suspected her of faking the symptoms to get attention. But then, lifting her blouse, he saw the dreaded tokens. She died the following night. Not long after, he visited "a widow of some sixty years of age, whom I met with at dinner, where she had eaten heartily of mutton, and filled besides her stomach with broth; after I had inquired into several particulars relating to her health, she affirmed herself to have never been better in her life." He took her pulse and found it to be racing. On her breast, he discovered a sprinkling of tokens. He marveled that "even after so good a dinner" she passed away that very evening. Boghurst wrote at length how to avoid dying of the plague, but in sum, he seems to put the most confidence in just this: "Cheerfulness and courage of heart and spirit did chiefly uphold some in this disease; verifying [Biblical King] Solomon's saying, viz., a merry heart doth good like a medicine, whereas melancholy and dejection of spirits was the overthrow of many."

Current historians, however, examining eyewitness accounts, parish records, letters, and other documents, conclude several things about the nature of the plague and how it struck. Stephen Porter, author of *The Great Plague,* notes that the death rate was higher among

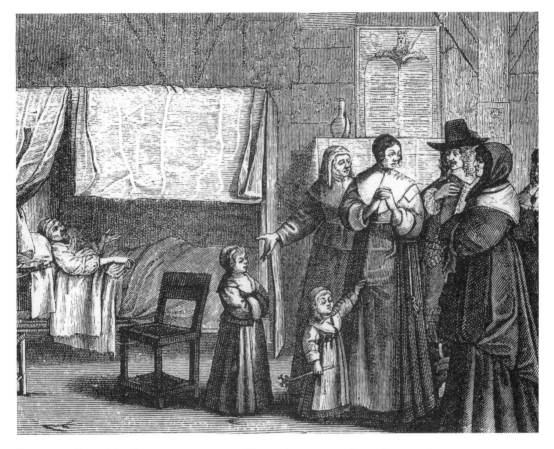

Doctors often visited patients at home if they were too sick to travel. The practice also helped contain illness where it lay. One of the more alarming symptoms of bubonic plague was the delirium and hysteria that struck its victims. Patients often caused even more harm to themselves and the uninfected public in their frenzy.

women. He points out that domestic servants were generally women, and they would have had to go into public places to buy provisions and run errands. The more people a person came in contact with, the greater his or her likelihood of contracting plague.

Also, the perception among Londoners in 1665 that the plague deserved the nickname "the Poors Plague" was correct. Historian Justin Champion compared burial registers with the Hearth Tax Records of 1660; the Hearth Tax taxed households' wealth or lack of it on the basis of the number of fireplaces. His conclusion: poverty and plague went hand in hand, almost parish by parish. "[T]he type of physical space inhabited, determined the type of mortality experienced," he wrote. "If you lived in

Cock and Key Alley rather than Chancery Lane, or in St. Botolph without Aldgate rather than St. Mary Colechurch you were more likely to contract the plague." He added, however, that living in one of the wealthier parts of town did not make anyone immune to the disease, as Samuel Pepys knew well.

Pepys, arriving by riverboat after meeting with the Duke of Albemarle about navy business, wrote on August 15 that "it was dark before I could get home, and so landed at Church-yard stairs, where, to my great trouble, I met a dead corpse of the plague, in the narrow alley just bringing down a little pair of stairs. But I thank God that I was not much disturbed at it. However, I shall beware of being late abroad again." About the same time, his friend John Evelyn, coming into the city on a similar errand, wrote in his diary, "I went all along the city and suburbs from Kent Street to St. James's, a dismal passage, and dangerous to see so many coffins exposed in the streets, now thin of people; the shops shut up, and all in mournful silence, not knowing whose turn it might be next."

Thomas Vincent also remarked on the city's quiet, deserted character. "Now [in August] there is a dismal solitude in London streets, every day looks like the face of a sabbath day, observed with greater solemnity than it used to be in the city. Now shops are shut in, people rare, and very few that walk about, insomuch that the grass begins to spring up in some places. . . . If any voice be heard, it is the groans of dying persons, breathing forth their last, and the funeral knells of them that are ready to be carried to their graves."

The Bills of Mortality published at the end of July had shown death rates many times greater than normal— 8,828 had died that month, 5,667 from plague. No one could have suspected that August and September would be far, far worse.

"More Cruel to One Another Than if We Are Dogs"

With much of the London population fled and dozens of dead carts roaming the streets, it was clear that the vibrancy of the noisy city and opulent Restoration court was no more. Could this be the vengeance wreaked by God against a wicked and sinful capital?

"But what greatly contributed to the loss of people thus shut up, was the wicked practices of nurses (for they are not to be mention'd but in the most bitter terms): these wretches, out of greediness to plunder the dead, would strangle their patients."

—Dr. Nathaniel Hodges, 1672

By August, the plague had been raging for nearly three months, and no doubt the psychological stress on Londoners must have been severe. On August 3, Pepys included in his diary a story he had heard. It seems Sir Anthony Browne, his brother, and some friends were traveling along a narrow street in a coach when they saw another coach coming in the other direction. "The brother being a young man,"

Pepys says, "and believing there might be some lady in it that would not be seen, and the way being narrow, he thrust his head out his own into her coach." What the young man saw made both him and the coachman shout in horror. In the coach was a half-dead young woman in a "sick dress," who "stunk mightily," on her way to a pest house for plague victims.

Worried citizens tried a number of different methods to avoid catching the plague. In market-places, merchants put bowls of disinfecting vinegar out and asked customers to drop their coins in, rather than risk touching their hands. In the post office in Cloak Lane, Dowgate, the daily fumigation of burn-ing a mixture of brimstone, saltpeter, and amber made the air so smoky that those working there could hardly see each other. Before a letter could be mailed out, it had to be waved over vinegar.

Living daily in the shadow of the plague and the suffering it caused drove some people to the point of despair. John Allin, a physician, wrote to a friend in the country, "Never did so many husbands and wives die together; never did so many parents carry their children with them to the grave, and go together to the same house under the earth, who had lived in the same house upon it. Now the nights are too short to bury the dead. . . . Death approacheth nearer and nearer, not many doors off, and the pit open daily within view of my chamber window. The Lord fit me and all of us for our last end!"

The pit that Allin refers to was a necessity that overburdened parishes were forced to resort to—a mass grave in which dozens of bodies could be buried at once. In the early days of the outbreak, churches were willing to accommodate families as best they could—even to the point of ignoring the city's Plague

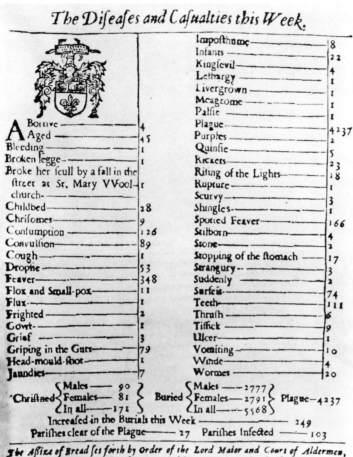

The Bill of Mortality faithfully recorded deaths and their causes. One page showed that 4,237 people died from the plague out of 5,568 total deaths that week. This information was important to the office of the Lord Mayor of London, who was responsible to contain such disasters.

Orders forbidding public funerals for health reasons. But now in August the urgent task of burying the dead became more important than respecting the feelings of the living. Churches dispensed with the niceties of a Christian burial. According to Defoe, "some blamed the churchwardens for suffering such a frightful thing . . . but time made it appear the churchwardens knew the condition of the parish better than they did."

As the month wore on, circumstances proved the churchwardens right. The first pit in the cemetery of St. Botolph Aldgate was dug in mid-August, for instance, received its first corpse on September 6, and within two weeks had been filled up with 1,114 bodies. Evelyn notes in his diary that the Bills of Mortality reported 5,000 deaths in London between August 8 and 15. Many parishes—especially in poor sections of the city where the death rates were highest—had neither the money, manpower, nor time to provide individual graves. The pit became a necessary evil.

The pits were about 40 feet long, 15 feet wide, and 18 feet deep—grave diggers could go no lower without hitting water—and the bearers of the dead carts put as many bodies into them as they could while still leaving a space for six feet of dirt on top as the law required. Defoe described a mass burial:

> The cart had in it sixteen or seventeen bodies; some were wrapped up in linen sheets, some in rags, some little other than naked, or so loose that what covering they had fell from them in the shooting out of the cart, and they fell quite naked among the rest; but the matter was not much to them, or the indecency much to anyone else, seeing they were all dead, and were to be huddled together into the common grave of mankind, as we may call it, for here was no difference made, but poor and rich went together; there was no other way of burials, neither was it possible there should, for coffins were not to be had for the prodigious numbers that fell in such a calamity as this.

Even such measures were not foolproof, however. Complaints about the pits and "noisome stenches arising from the great number of dead" buried in the New Churchyard, for example, forced the city to issue orders requiring bones and coffin boards sticking out to be burned, and a fresh layer of earth thrown on top.

So much exposure to death, added to by pressure

from the fear of one's own death, created a macabre atmosphere in the city, coarsening Londoners' behavior toward each other. Parish officials found it harder and harder to hire enough good people to do the grisly work that needed to be done, either because dependable workers had died or no one wanted the jobs.

As a result, terrible stories of ghoulish behavior circulated about the city, many of them true. A bearer

This rough drawing depicts two workers, a grave digger and a death cart driver, who were kept unusually busy as London's death rate skyrocketed during the summer of 1665.

of a dead cart, said Defoe, within earshot of him and his frightened siblings, seized a dead child by the ankle and held it up to the window above, shouting drunkenly, "Faggots o' wood for the fire: five for sixpence!" One Londoner complained that the crews were generally "very idle base living men and very rude" given to loudly "swearing and cursing." More than one burial party—excusing themselves by saying the dead wouldn't care—stripped off the costly linen shrouds from bodies and resold them. Searchers, an increasing number of whom were drunks, let it be known that they would not report plague, thereby sparing a family quarantine—but only for the right price. Unscrupulous warders guarding households extorted bribes from those wanting to pass food and medicine to friends and relatives inside.

And the "wicked practices of nurses (for they are not to be mention'd but in the most bitter terms)," wrote Dr. Hodges disgustedly, "these wretches, out of greediness to plunder the dead, would strangle their patients, and charge it to the distemper in their throats; others would secretly convey the pestilential taint from sores of the infected to those who were well," as a way of giving themselves work.

Nor were examples of cruelty and lawlessness all on the side of parish workers, either. It was known that some quarantined families broke out by attacking or fooling the warders. Some lowered a noose over the neck of a sleeping guard, then yanked him off his feet and left him hanging while everyone fled. Others sent a warder on an errand for food or medicine, then picked the lock while he was away. One citizen left a maid ill with plague in her attic bedroom while he chiseled a hole in a wall and led his family through it. Another poured gunpowder on a warder, ignited it, and as the man roasted in agony kicked out a first-floor window and escaped. Thieves plundered vacant houses, and in one instance burglars were caught making off with their loot in two coffins.

Gradually, the system of quarantining households broke down. Concerns arose over the plight of persons desperate to feed themselves or to get treatment for loved ones. Pepys, serving on a special committee investigating violations of quarantine, added to his diary the story of a "very able citizen in Gracious Street, a saddler, who had buried all the rest of his children of the plague, and himself and his wife now being shut up and in despair of escaping, did desire only to save the life of this little child." The child was lowered, naked, into the arms of a friend, who dressed it in fresh clothes and took it to safety. The committee, Pepys said, decided to do nothing about the case.

An even more compelling reason for putting a stop to quarantine was that shutting up houses raised the mortality rate of those trapped inside and increased the parish's economic hardship. Historian Stephen Porter used the parish of St. Giles, Cripplegate, as an example: "Felix Bragg, his wife and daughter were buried on the same day; four children from one family were interred within six days; and in the space of four days the parish clerk recorded the burials of Thomas Crawley, his wife, son, two daughters and a journeyman who worked for him." By the middle of August, wrote Porter, "the numbers infected in St. Giles, Cripplegate were so great that the parish could not deal with the problem and so stopped confining plague suspects to their houses, 'lest the sick & poore should be famished within dores.'"

With quarantine measures eroding, the citizenry was both relieved on the one hand, but still more anxious on the other. People walked in the middle of the streets, speaking to no one and trying not to breathe odors from households touched by plague. Pepys went to the Exchange, where men of business heard the latest news and looked after their affairs, but he too spoke to no one. Public funerals, which the city seemed unable or unwilling to stop, were a sore point among many. Despite Plague Orders forbidding them, Pepys reported seeing a procession of 40 or 50 mourners.

The remorselessness of the plague—nearly 5,000 died the week ending August 29—meant big business for "chymists and quacks" and "wicked impostors" as Dr. Hodges called them. From buying powered toad to powdered unicorn's horn, from wearing amulets soaked in toad poison to sucking on a gold coin, Londoners tried anything they could to avoid plague. A few even deliberately contracted syphilis because it was said to bring immunity from plague. Dozens of pamphlets appeared, "some trash or other under the disguise of a pompous title," Hodges said, each one recommending a special cure. A pamphlet called *The Plague's Approved Physician* advised, "If there do a botch appear: Take a pigeon and pluck the feathers off her tail, very bare, and set her tail to the sore, and she will draw out the venom till she die; then take another and set to likewise, continuing so till all the venom be drawn out, which you shall see by the pigeons, for they will die with the venom as long as there is any in [the tumor]: also a chicken or hen is very good."

Yet running against the tide of hysteria and brutality were the calm, careful actions of many citizens, chief among them doctors like Hodges and Boghurst, who moved about the city ministering to the sick and the dying. The costume of a doctor in times of contagion

Doctors caring for plague patients typically dressed in a large cape and hat, carried a type of walking stick, and wore a primitive form of gas mask. The "beak" was stuffed with herbs to protect the doctor from contagion.

was a cape, a black hat, a brightly colored cane, and a mask with a beak that made the healer look more like a huge, sinister bird than someone on a mission of mercy. The beak was a sort of gas mask stuffed with herbs that was supposed to filter out the taint of sickness. It's unknown whether Hodges or Boghurst wore the outfit.

In *Loimologia,* Hodges detailed his practices during the plague. He rose early every morning and took a dose of nutmeg. Attending first to "private concerns in my family," he then went into a large room "where crowds of citizens used to be in waiting for me." After spending two or three hours examining patients and making recommendations, he went directly to the homes of the sick, careful to arrive cool and unhurried and keeping his mind, he said, "as composed as possible." Returning home, he had a glass of sack (white wine) before dinner—a practice he recommended to patients, too—and then after dinner returned to see patients in the waiting room until nine at night.

Boghurst was equally fearless and compassionate in the face of the disease. Not only did he dress the sores of the afflicted and give them medicines to make them sweat, but

> [I] held them up in their beds to keep them from strangling and choking half an hour together, commonly suffered their breathing in my face several times when they were dying, ate and drank with them, especially those that had sores, sat down by their bed sides and upon their beds discoursing with them an hour together if I had time, and stayed by them to see the manner of their death, and closed up their mouth and eyes (for they died with their mouth and eyes very much open and staring); then if people had nobody to help them (for help was scarce at such a time and place) I helped to lay them forth out of the bed and afterwards into the coffin, and last of all accompanying them to the grave.

As August turned into September the plague showed no signs of slackening—in fact the darkest days were just ahead. Relentlessly, the disease claimed an average of

Doctors were the main force in fighting the disease, but not everyone put their total trust in these learned men of science. The number of people escaping from their quarantined houses gradually increased until the city finally suspended the practice of isolation.

6,000 lives a week—probably more because the deaths of Jews and Protestant Nonconformists went unrecorded. Simon Patrick, rector of St. Paul's, Covent Garden, wrote to a lady friend concerned about his safety: "I suppose you think I intend to stay here still; though I understand by your question you would not have me. But, my friend, what am I better than another? Somebody must stay here. . . . If you can convince me, that I may, with good conscience go, you may think it will be acceptable. But I know not upon what grounds you will make it good."

Quiet acts of heroism and courage took place all over the city, though none so remarkable as one that occurred far outside the city in the little town of Eyam in Derbyshire. Plague arrived in Eyam hidden in old clothes sent from London. Prompted by their rector, the Rev. William Mompesson, the villagers sealed themselves off from the outside world to prevent the spread of the disease to their neighbors. About 260 of the 800 or so inhabitants died. An annual memorial service is held on the last Sunday of August near the limestone rock where Mompesson preached to the villagers, persuading them that their sacrifice would not go unrewarded.

Pepys, his nerves frayed by the summer-long siege of the worst plague in the city's history, shows signs of strain in his diary. Passing a farmhouse where a coffin had lain in the open uncollected for hours, he complained about people's insensitivity, saying "this disease [is] making us more cruel to one another than if we are dogs." Later, he jotted down in a disjointed way scenes he could not forget:

My meeting dead corpses of the plague, carried to be buried close to me at noonday through the city in Fenchurch Street. To see a person sick of the sores, carried close by me by Gracechurch in a hackney coach. My finding the Angel Tavern at the lower end of Tower Hill shut up, and more than that the alehouse at Tower Stairs, and more than that, that the person was then dying of the plague when I was last there a little while ago at night. To hear that poor Payne, my waiter, had buried a child and is dying himself. To hear that a laborer I sent but the other day to Dagenhams to know how they did there, is dead of the plague, and that one of my own watermen, that carried me daily, fell sick as soon as he had landed me on Friday morning last, when I had been all night upon the water . . . and is now dead of the plague. . . . And lastly that both my servants W. Hewer and Tom Edwards have lost their fathers, both in St. Sepulchre parish, of the plague this week, do put me into great apprehension and melancholy and with good reason.

By mid-September, Pepys devoutly hoped that the rumor beginning to circulate was true: the plague was showing signs of having run its course.

Some people lit bonfires to fumigate neighborhoods in the fall of 1665, as had been tried once before during an outbreak. The colder autumn weather caused a decrease in the number of rats, fleas, and accompanying infectious bacteria. Fewer people therefore contracted and died from the plague.

End to the Season of Death

"It frighted me indeed to go through the church more than I thought it could have done, to see so many graves lie so high upon the churchyards where people have been buried of plague."

—Samuel Pepys, January 30, 1666

Perhaps people's hopes that the plague would end soon were inspired by nature's unexpected bounty. According to the Bills of Mortality for September, almost 7,000 were dying each week. Yet the autumn harvest—like a sign of compassion by heaven—was plentiful. Fruit was so inexpensive that the poor feasted more often on apples, pears, cherries, plums, mulberries, raspberries, and strawberries than many could remember for a long time. The scent of new-mown hay reached the city center from the surrounding fields.

In fact, London smelled almost unnaturally sweet. Backyard gardens left unattended grew wild, and vegetables rotted and fermented in the sun. Residents of the stricken city who ventured outside carried spices and flowers to inhale to fend off plague—"a pocketful of posies," as the children's rhyme went. "Such as go abroad," the College of Physicians recommended, "shall do well to carry rue, angelica, masterwort, myrrhe, scordium, or water germander, wormwood, valerian, or setwall root, Virginian snake root, or zedoary in their hands to smell to; and of those they may hold or chew a little in their mouths as they go in the streets." But so few people went outdoors, except on errands, that the streets were deserted, packed down smooth and dry. Hardly a dog or cat could be seen poking about the alleyways and passages, because nearly all had been caught and killed.

Householders who could afford it burned incense—frankincense, amber, cedar, bay leaves, and rosemary to perfume the air and hopefully to erase contagion. City officials, helpless to slow the arrests of "Sergeant Death," as clergyman Thomas Vincent referred to the plague, decided to try fumigating the whole metropolis. Soldiers stacked sweet-smelling wood in front of every third home and set it afire. Some complained about the expense, but no one seems to have worried whether it was wise to set bonfires in the timber-built city. Bonfires had been tried once before during an outbreak. Perhaps people took comfort in the blazes burning all day and all night, tended by watchmen. But then on the third night, a heavy downpour doused the wood and put the fires out.

The number of plague deaths dipped briefly after that, suggesting that outdoor fumigating had done the trick after all. Rector Simon Patrick took it as a good sign when he saw a group of about 30 people walking near the riverbank carrying white sticks. They were plague survivors from a pest house on their way to see a justice for certificates of health.

A more likely explanation for the drop in deaths was that the heavy rains had washed the kennels, or gutters, clear and rinsed the sewers. The city was just unusually clean.

But despite rumors that the plague was running down, many who had fled in the spring judged it too early to return. In mid-September, St. Bartholomew's Hospital remained so short-handed that the hospital's governors sent letters to Doctors Henry Boone and Thomas Woodhall instructing them to return immediately or pay someone else to do the work. Boone sent a note of refusal, saying he "desired to be excused to do that service." Woodhall paid someone else, Thomas Turpin, to substitute. But Turpin arrived at the hospital, sized up the situation and quit, vaguely explaining that "the business was too hot for him to act." So the staff carried on with one doctor, Thomas Gray; an apothecary to mix medicines, Francis Bernard; a matron or head nurse, Margaret Blue; and 15 nuns.

During the third week of September, the sun shone hotly every day. Plague deaths shot up over 7,000 as the flea population exploded in the heat. A clerk writing at his desk collapsed, close to death, his signature trailing off into an illegible inky smudge. For September, the Bill of Mortality listed 30,899 deaths—the highest monthly figure of the year—nearly half of them in the poor parishes. Bands of orphans roamed the streets, begging by day, and sleeping together in camps under the Thames River bridges at night.

Finally in early October the weather turned cooler, and predictably there was a steady and long-awaited decrease in deaths. Londoners took advantage of the decline to flock to the churches. They spilled out the front doors for services, wanting to hear a reason, an acceptable explanation, for this scourge more deadly than any recorded since the Black Death of the 1300s. In many of the pulpits were Protestant Nonconformist ministers, who had been preaching ever since some of their Anglican, or Church of England, colleagues had abandoned the city in the spring. "Now there is such a vast concourse of people in the churches, where these ministers are to be found," wrote Nonconformist minister Vincent, "that they cannot many times come near the pulpit doors for the press, but are forced to climb over the pews to them . . . such eager looks, such open ears, such greedy attention, as if every word would be eaten, which dropped from the mouths of ministers."

Though some clergymen offered sermons of reassurance, urging survivors to express their gratitude to God and not to judge those who had perished, others could not resist delivering a hard lesson. Vincent, for instance, believed the plague had rightly terrified "the old drunkards, and swearers, and unclean persons, [who] see many fellow-sinners fall before their faces, expecting every hour themselves to be smitten." Church of England ministers still at their posts seized the opportunity to preach politics and scold their critics. They thundered that the epidemic was the price of disobedience to authority. Just as the Israelites who rebelled against Moses and Aaron were punished by God with plague, so the arrogance of those who

The Bible describes a world destroyed by flood and many epidemics. For instance, the Israelites who rebelled against Moses and Aaron were punished by God with plague. According to one of the texts, Revelation, the world will next be destroyed (and thereby cleansed yet again) by fire. Little did the survivors of the plague in 1665 know that the fire was to be their next disaster.

questioned the legitimacy of the Church of England—Catholics, Puritans, backsliding Protestants—had been answered in the same way.

Unfortunately, some worshippers listening patiently in congregations around the city drew only one conclusion, regardless of what was said. They bragged to neighbors that they hadn't caught the plague because they were religious and God-fearing. God had spared them as a sign of favor—it was that simple.

As the weather continued to turn colder, "people grew more healthful, and such a different face was put upon the public," noted Dr. Hodges. The mystery of plague defied understanding, but one thing was certain—heavy frost cut short the season of death. Following a cold snap at the end of November, the number of weekly deaths fell to several hundred. Samuel Pepys's father wrote to him in a happy frame of mind, saying that "he saw York's [the city] wagon go again this week to London, and [it] was full of passengers." In December, "they crowded back as thick as they [had] fled," Dr. Hodges said.

Not everyone found himself welcomed home again in the city, however. Defoe described the treatment given to long-absent doctors and clergymen who resurfaced at the end of the awful year 1665, when the coast was clear:

> Great was the reproach thrown on those physicians who left their patients during sickness, and now they came to town again nobody cared to employ them. They were called deserters, and frequently bills were set upon their doors and written, 'Here is a doctor to be let [rented],' so that several of those physicians were fain for a while to sit still and look about them, or at least remove their dwellings, and set up in new places and among new acquaintance. The like was the case with the clergy, whom the people were indeed very abusive to, writing verses and scandalous reflections upon them, setting upon the church-door, 'Here is a pulpit to be let,' or sometimes 'to be sold,' which was worse.

Nor were other people coming back to London correct in assuming that the plague had left the city once and for all, fading away like the old year itself. Hodges, who had spent practically every waking hour for the last several months coping with the disease's horrors,

Two doctors examine the body of a patient dead with plague, attempting to learn the cause of the disease from an autopsy. The number of cases had dropped dramatically by December 1665 and people returned to the city, crowding together once again. The close conditions caused a small resurgence of the epidemic.

watched incredulously as "those citizens, who before were afraid even of their friends and relations, would without fear venture into houses and rooms where infected persons had but a little before breathed their last: nay . . . many went into the beds where persons had died before they were even cold, or cleansed from the stench of the diseased." Perhaps it says something about the human spirit that people took up again so bravely where they had left off, but many paid for it, too. The number of plague deaths spiked suddenly in December at Christmastime, exactly a year after

Hodges had diagnosed an early case that proved to be the beginning of London's nightmare.

In his house, at least, Pepys argued with his wife about her "desiring a maid yet, before the plague is quite over," insisting that he would not risk his family by adding a servant "before it be safe." But four days later, on the very last day of the year, December 31, with a cooler head he took stock of his affairs, balanced out his account books, and felt very pleased. By remaining in the vicinity of the city and volunteering for various emergency duties, he had tripled his income. In high spirits, he boasted, "I have never lived so merrily (besides that I never got so much) as I have done this plague time."

Nor did his loyalty go unnoticed by King Charles. Near the end of January 1666, Pepys visited Hampton Court, where the royal family was preparing to return to London. The king "came to me of himself," Pepys wrote proudly in his diary, "and told me, 'Mr. Pepys,' says he, 'I do give you thanks for your good service all this year, and I assure you I am very sensible of it.'"

Feelings of relief and gratitude must have been common among survivors of the plague of 1665 as winter came on. Plague's power seemed to freeze with the cold temperatures as fleas and rats died. But a sense of grief must have hung heavily over the city, too. A slow massacre had taken place in London month after month, from May to December. Historian Stephen Porter estimates the number of plague deaths between 70,000 and 75,000, and perhaps as many as 100,000 because some religious sects—the Jews and the Quakers mainly—held their own burial services and the deaths went unrecorded in the parish registers.

Returning to his usual church for services, St. Olave's, for the first time in months, Pepys was shocked to see "so many graves lie so high upon the churchyards where people have been buried of the plague." Even today, the doors of some parish churches in the center of London are slightly below ground level because the graveyards are over-filled with plague dead. "I was much troubled at it," Pepys said of his visit to the churchyard, "and do not think to go through it again a good while."

Southwarke

Fire!

From a source not completely known, the Great Fire of London began on September 2 and burned for four days. Only a few people died but at least 80,000 lost their homes. Afterward, houses, businesses, public buildings, and ancient landmarks like Old St. Paul's Cathedral were gone forever.

"A small spark, from an unknown cause, for want of timely care, increased to such a flame, that neither the tears of the people, nor the profusion of their Thames, could extinguish [it]."

—Dr. Nathaniel Hodges, 1672

With the arrival of spring in 1666, Londoners wondered whether plague would erupt as it had the year before. And in fact, the number of plague deaths in April and May averaged about 30 a week—higher than normal, but the city remained calm. In previous years, this figure might have caused alarm. But by comparison—remember that 7,000 had died each week during

September 1665—the totals in the Bills of Mortality were greeted cheerfully. In mid-July, plague deaths peaked at 51, but they were scattered over 21 parishes—nothing like the concentration of hundreds of deaths in just a single parish when the plague was at full force.

On August 9, 1666, Pepys ran into his friend and fellow-diarist John Evelyn in a London street. Evelyn told him of "the sad condition at this very day at Deptford for the plague"—the town where Evelyn lived. But Pepys only mentions the information in passing, whereas during the rest of August he devotes whole paragraphs in his diary to talking about two of his favorite hobbies—book collecting and amateur science. By autumn, plague was no longer a terror; it was just part of conversation. It was only one of a dozen life-threatening but common illnesses that Londoners coped with, such as smallpox, "spotted fever," "teeth and worms," rickets, cancer, scurvy, and consumption (tuberculosis).

Unfortunately, London was about to be visited by yet another calamity. In the early morning hours of Sunday, September 2, while Pepys's maids were staying up late, one of them woke him and Elizabeth to "tell us of a great fire they saw in the city." Pepys put on his robe and looked out the window. He could see signs of fire about a quarter mile away to the west. This fire would soon become the infamous four-day inferno that engulfed the city center of London, destroying it.

Earlier that evening, about 10 o'clock, the king's baker, Thomas Farrinor, had turned in for the night above his shop in Pudding Lane. Around midnight, he needed a candle for some reason and checked to see that his oven was out. No embers glowed inside, he later told a board of inquiry. But then two hours later he and his son and daughter "felt themselves almost choked with smoke." He rushed to the top of the stairs and saw flames shooting up the steps. The blaze was not near the oven, nor was it in the woodpile beside the house. With the way downstairs cut off, the three Farrinors clambered out on to the roof, pleading with their maid to follow them. But her fear of heights was greater than her fear of fire, and she turned away from the window, disappearing into the smoke and becoming the Great Fire of London's first victim. The baker and his children inched their way along the gutter to a neighbor's house and safety.

The fire, at roof level, leaped on a strong wind across to Fish Street Hill and the Star Inn. Fire was always a threat in timber-built London. To seal the dry joints of windows, doorframes, walls, and roofs, builders used inflammable pitch and tar. Now, with the right conditions, structures ignited like tinder. Within minutes, the galleries lining the interior courtyard of the Star Inn were rolling with flames. Sparks flew the short distance to the warehouses on Thames Street, which were stocked with oil, brandy, wine, tallow, and other combustibles.

Someone thought the Lord Mayor, Thomas Bludworth, ought to be alerted. Bludworth arrived on the scene about an hour after the fire had broken out, unimpressed and apparently annoyed at having been rousted out of bed. "Pish! A woman might piss it out," he said. This rude comment would prove to be spectacularly wrong.

To fight the fire, volunteer brigades lined up to receive equipment from storage, usually the tower of the parish church. Hand-held brass squirters were distributed, as were leather buckets, ladders, and long poles with hooks for pulling down flaming pieces of wood or straw. A few parishes had primitive fire engines—big barrels of water on carts that could be hauled into the street. Water was also available from public wells fed by wood and lead pipes beneath the streets. The volunteers got to work, throwing buckets of water on the flames. Already St. Margaret's Church, Fish Street Hill, was ablaze; some warehouses on Thames Street belched oily clouds of smoke; and above the heads of the firefighters, swirling streams of glowing embers flew like pollen, carrying fire to other rooftops.

Then, sometime during the night, certainly before sunrise, the battle was effectively lost. "Fire! Fire! Fire! doth resound in every street," reported the *London Gazette*, "some starting out of their sleep and peeping through the windows half-dressed. Some in night dresses rushing wildly about the streets crying piteously and praying to God for assistance, women carrying children in their arms and the men looking quite bewildered. Many cripples were also seen hobbling about not knowing which way to go to get free from the flames which were raging all round them."

The fire, reaching the riverbank, burned the pumping houses near London Bridge. Water stopped flowing into the heart of the city. Aided by the wind, the blaze then drifted back toward the city center, fueling itself street by street. The best thing would have been to pull down houses in the fire's path to try to create a firebreak—a cleared area the fire could not jump—but the Lord Mayor hesitated. Who would pay for the repairs? he wondered aloud, recalling a medieval law that whoever caused destruction to a house was liable for the cost.

Shortly after Pepys rose at seven o'clock Sunday morning, one of his maids told him she had heard that

300 houses had been lost. Alarmed, he went to the Tower of London, accompanied by the young son of a friend of his, and mounted the stairs to the top. What he saw was an "infinite great fire on this and on the other side" of London Bridge. He quickly went down to the river and hired a boat to take him to Whitehall, the king's London residence. Passing under London Bridge, he saw pigeons flapping above him with burning wings. Incredible as it seems, Pepys turned out to be the first person to inform Charles II and his brother James, the Duke of York (later King James II), about the extent of the fire. Listening with dismay, Charles directed Pepys to tell the Lord Mayor to "spare no houses, but to pull down before the fire every way."

Returning to the city center by carriage, through streets crowded with gawkers and fleeing people, Pepys managed to locate the Lord Mayor near the blaze. Bludworth, a bureaucrat losing his nerve in the face of a terrible event, dabbed the perspiration from his neck with a handkerchief as he listened to Pepys's orders from the king, then bleated, "Lord! What can I do? I am spent: people will not obey me. I have been pulling down houses; but the fire overtakes us faster than we can do it." Then he hurried away to "go and refresh himself, having been up all night." The *London Gazette* commented bitterly, "What a confusion! The Lord Mayor of the city came with his officers, and London so famous for its wisdom can find neither hands nor brains to prevent its utter ruin. London must fall to the ground in ashes and who can prevent it?"

But in fact, no one living had ever seen a catastrophe like the one unfolding. No one was certain how to resist it. Walking through the streets, Pepys said, "with one's face in the wind, you were almost burned with a shower of fire drops." The spectacle of one of the great capitals of civilization burning had an otherworldliness about it: "Never was there the like Sabbath in London," the *Gazette* declared. "Many churches were in flames that day; God seemed to come down and preach himself in them."

By midday Sunday, panicky Londoners were throwing their goods into the river, unable to flee via blocked streets. They trotted along the banks, keeping an eye on their bobbing bundles, hoping to intercept them safely downstream. Adding to their fears were rumors that the fire had been set by the Dutch—England was still at war with Holland—and that a French and Catholic army of 4,000 was marching toward London to finish the job. Someone on horseback rode through the streets shouting, "Arm! Arm!"

At London's Westminster School, 15-year-old William Taswell could barely wait for Sunday morning services to end so he could see firsthand what was happening. He hurried down to the river and saw boats nearly swamped with people and their belongings. Turning into the city, he saw Londoners, maddened by rumors that foreigners had set the city on fire, taking vengeance. "A blacksmith, in my presence, meeting an innocent Frenchman walking along the street, felled him instantly to the ground with an iron bar." Blood streamed down the man's legs to his ankles. Then Taswell came upon a crowd throwing the belongings of another Frenchmen into the street, after which they pulled down his house, jeering that he meant to start it on fire anyway. In a field, Taswell's brother saw a Frenchman nearly torn apart because a mob thought the tennis balls he was lugging in a chest were "balls of fire."

Word of the fire reached John Evelyn in Deptford, and Sunday evening after dinner, he went with his wife

Some people self-righteously believed they had been personally chosen by God to survive the Great Plague, but no one's house was safe from the Great Fire of London. Rather than organizing to fight the fire, people instead carried off their own possessions and helplessly surveyed the inferno-like landscape.

and son as close to London as they dared, "where we beheld that dismal spectacle, the whole city in flames near the water side." As darkness fell, said the *London Gazette*, "Many were upon their knees in the night, pouring out tears before the Lord; interceding for poor London in the day of its calamity; but all in vain."

On Monday, September 3, the king and the Duke

The Thames River bordering London was a huge part of life in the city. The river served as a sewer, a trade route, and as a means of escape. City dwellers tried to escape the fire by boat, while others attempted to save their possessions by throwing them into the river and retrieving them downstream.

of York took control of the fire fighting. A main headquarters was set up with fire posts scattered around the perimeter of the city, which served as reporting stations. Each fire post had 35 soldiers assigned to it under an officer and 100 local civilians under the parish constable, or sheriff. The duke rode up and down the length of the city on horseback, accompanied by an armed guard, urging the populace to stay calm. Maintaining calm would be critical, because the king and his advisors had decided the only way to defeat the fire was to use gunpowder to blow up buildings in its path.

Through the gates of the city, from the surrounding countryside, men driving carts and wagons began arriving with offers of assistance to help Londoners evacuate. Sometimes charity was the only motive; other times, it was greed. Faced with losing treasures they had managed to salvage, desperate city dwellers paid ridiculously high fees to get their belongings at least to Moorfields, a vast open area which was turning into a refugee camp. William Taswell's family found out how easily "downright plunderers" operated. His parents gratefully accepted the help of men posing as porters, or luggage carriers, who promptly carried off their belongings and were never seen again.

Meanwhile, the fire was creating unearthly scenes and strangely fascinating sounds. The constant roar of flaming buildings collapsing sounded like surf crashing against an invisible rocky shore. The timbers of a church, standing without roof or walls, glowed bright gold "in the shape of a bow, and a fearful bow it was!" said the *Gazette*. According to John Evelyn, on Monday night, darkness never arrived. Until dawn, it was light as day for 10 miles around the city.

Then, on the third day, the tragedy of the Great Fire seemed to climax like the beginning of the third act of a play. "On Tuesday the fire burned up the very bowels of London," reported the *Gazette* flatly, "from Bow-lane, Bread-street, Friday-street, and Old Change the flames came up almost together." Like a piece of paper lit at one of its bottom corners, London was being consumed by fire burning in an ever-widening arc, up through the center of the city and out toward the walls. Until now, Old St. Paul's Cathedral looked like it might be spared from the flames creeping nearer and nearer and encircling it. Perhaps the cathedral's vast lead roof and thick stone walls would help it defy the onslaught of embers and heat. Booksellers along Paternoster Row certainly hoped so. The day before they had packed their inventories, thousands of books, into little Faith Church beneath the building.

All day Tuesday, September 4, Old St. Paul's stood untouched. But boards had been left lying on top of the roof during repairs, and tongues of flames began appearing up there as crowds below watched. The 500-year-old wooden joists supporting the roof ignited. Eerily, the great sheets of whitened metal covering the roof turned molten and began to puddle. "Now the lead melts and runs," said clergyman Thomas Vincent, watching, "as if it had been snow before the sun, and with a great noise fall on the pavement, and break through into Faith Church underneath, and great flakes of stone scale, and peel off strangely from the side of the walls." An old man ran inside to retrieve his blanket and perished.

As streams of liquid lead splashed down over the walls, it ran into the cracks between blocks of stones, where it cooled. Mortar gave way under the strain and stones exploded. Hundred-pound blocks shot into the air and landed crashing on the superheated pavement. The booksellers' wares, heaped in Faith Church, stoked the fire and the floor of Old St. Paul's split. A funerary bust of the poet John Donne slipped down through the floor into the basement, where it was later recovered. His face emerging from a shroud is the only important artifact from Old St. Paul's that survives. The cathedral continued to burn all night.

Eighty thousand Londoners were homeless by Tuesday night. Without insurance—it was a business that did not yet exist—nearly all were ruined. Moor-fields appeared to be occupied by an army that had brought its furniture along. Warehouses belonging to

Public and privately-owned structures all over the city were pulled down and blown up intentionally in an attempt to break the progress of the fire. But Old St. Paul's Cathedral, a 500-year-old landmark, was a symbol of the city itself. Unfortunately the church caught fire on the third day, and its lead roof melted off.

wealthy merchants fell in the Thames River and drifted with the current like ships on fire.

At dawn, Wednesday, the wind dropped a little. Fire-fighting efforts, especially the practice of demolishing houses to create firebreaks, either by pulling them down or blowing them up, began to take hold. Like a battlefront, however, the blaze still had to be fought at various points along its line in the city. Late in the day, the fire seemed to be making a fresh assault toward Middle Temple Hall, one of several buildings connected with the law courts. The Duke of York arrived on the scene with some of his advisors. Surveying the situation, the duke ordered the Paper House to be blown up. Suddenly, a young lawyer came hurrying out to explain to the future king that it was against the rules to use gunpowder on the grounds. One of the duke's men, Mr. Germaine, the Master of the Horse, was so incensed by this stupidity that he beat the young man then and there with a staff. "There is no hope of knowing who this lawyer is, but the hope that he will bring an action of battery against Mr. Germaine," sniffed a complainer in a letter to Lord Scudamore.

Thursday morning, with the fire finally under control, William Taswell set out to see what had become of Old St. Paul's. What had been the city's most important religious monument was a broken hulk of stone, minus roof, windows, and pieces of its walls. Taswell noticed that the smoldering ground was still so hot it nearly scorched his shoes. The bells in the tower had melted, dropping splotches of iron everywhere. They were round like coins, and Taswell picked up a few to put in his pocket as keepsakes. Leaning against the east wall was a figure. Taswell drew closer. It was the body of an old woman who had sheltered herself against the famous cathedral, probably believing it would protect her. "Her clothes were burnt, and every limb reduced to coal," Taswell said. He headed home, finding on the way a helmet and sword in some ruins, which he put on and wore like an explorer wandering through a strange landscape.

"London Was, But Is No More"

The ruins of London after the fire. Many French and Dutch citizens living in London were under suspicion of setting the fire and terrorized because of their nationality. A 26-year-old French silversmith, Robert Hubert, was eventually charged with and hanged for setting the blaze.

"London was, but is no more."

—John Evelyn, 1666

The fire had destroyed about four-fifths of the city, including roughly 13,200 houses, 90 parish churches, and nearly 50 livery company, or trade, halls—the Barber-Surgeon's Hall, Goldsmith's Hall, Plumber's Hall, Dyer's Hall, and so on. In addition, three city gates burned, as did the Royal Exchange, the Custom House, the Newgate jail for men, and four bridges. In all, the fire had charred an area of more than 430 acres, most of it inside the city walls. Pepys's house in Seething Lane was left untouched, although he had taken the precaution of burying some of his valuables, including his best wine and parmesan cheese. The fire didn't come near Evelyn's house in Deptford, either. It was too far away.

Historians wonder about what was lost. No plays written in Shakespeare's hand have ever been found. Perhaps they burned. We have two eyewitness diaries of those times, by Pepys and Evelyn—how many others were turned to ash? By accident, the booksellers of Paternoster Row made a bonfire of the most important works of the day by piling them underneath Old St. Paul's. What authors have been permanently forgotten because their best efforts were incinerated on Tuesday, September 4, 1666? No doubt hundreds of paintings hanging on the walls of homes curled up and caught fire too, enough portraits of people to fill a theater. Artists in those days used bitumen, an oil-base shellac, to protect their canvases. Little did they know that by coating their works with it they were priming them to burn one day like gas-soaked rags.

Yet in spite of the fire's devastation, only four persons in London are known to have died—Farrinor's maid in Pudding Lane where the fire began; the old man who went into Old St. Paul's to get his blanket; the old woman William Taswell found beside the east wall of the cathedral; and a watchmaker in Shoe Lane. Days after the fire, five more people accidentally died by falling into cellars while rummaging through debris.

Shortly after the fire, King Charles II rode among the homeless in Moorfields. Estimates are that 100,000 homeless were camped there, though Evelyn put the figure at 200,000. Describing them, he wrote, "People of all ranks and degrees dispersed and lying along by their heaps of what they could save from the fire, deploring their loss; and though ready to perish for hunger or destitution, yet not asking one penny for relief, which to me appeared a stranger sight than any I had yet beheld." King Charles assured them anyway that relief was on the way—hundreds of pounds of free bread, most of it taken from the navy's storehouses. He also emphasized that the fire was the hand of God and not an act of sabotage. He could defend them against any enemy and would live and die with them.

But even the mention of foreign enemies may have rekindled fears in the king's exhausted and dispirited subjects. Evelyn described how the rumor of an enemy army marching on the city resurfaced somehow and inspired a new wave of panic, even after the king's proclamation that things were well in hand:

> In the midst of all this calamity and confusion, there was, I know not how, an alarm begun that the French and Dutch, with whom we were now in hostility, were not only landed, but even entering the city. There was, in truth, some days before, great suspicion of those two nations joining; and now, that they had been the occasion [cause] of firing the town. This report did so terrify, that on a sudden there was such an uproar and tumult, that they ran from their goods, and taking what weapons they could come at, they could not be stopp'd from falling on some of those nations [Dutch and French persons living in London], whom they casually met, without sense or reason. The clamor and peril grew so excessive, that it made the whole court amaz'd, and they did with infinite pains and great difficulty reduce and appease the people, sending troops of soldiers and guards to cause them to return into the fields again, where they were watch'd all this night.

The stay in Moorfields by a third of London's population did not last long, in any case. As soon as they were able, many of the homeless decamped to live with relatives in the suburbs, though others returned to the city to see what they could salvage. It was an astonishing and discouraging landscape, made worse by the stench coming from still-burning warehouses sending dark billowing clouds into the air. Evelyn took his own survey of the damage and came upon strange sights—public wells boiling; stone columns and walls turned the color and texture of salt; chains, prison gates, locks, and bars melted. Many houses had fallen into their own cellars and were burning down to ash—nothing would be worth rescuing.

Still, life went on. The *London Gazette* carried notices intended to help readers get on with their day-to-day business: "The General Post-office is for the present held at the two Black Pillars in Bridges Street, over against the Fleece Tavern, Covent Garden, till a more convenient place can be found in London." And "[a]lso Alderman Meynell and Alderman Backwell, with diverse others of Lumbard Street, being likewise preserved in their estates, do intend to settle in a few days in or near Broard Street."

The helpful writers of the *Gazette* also reminded patriots not to overlook their blessings. The fire had not destroyed the king's stores of war kept in the Tower of London, nor had it reached the naval supply depot, either. God had not deprived England of the ability to keep fighting the Dutch and the French at least, or delivered the city into the hands of the enemy.

Despite this optimism, the citizens of London and its government were eager to affix blame for the Great Fire of London. Even though King Charles had pledged to the tens of thousands of homeless Londoners camped in Moorfields that the burning was not the work of saboteurs—he had personally questioned several suspects—a rumor continued that secret powers were at fault. Some recalled a prophecy in 1641 by Mother

Shipton that forecasted London's destruction, (Shipton was a fortune-teller whose pointed black hat and Puritan dress later became the model for Halloween witches). Others believed the French seer Nostradamus had also predicted the event in 1555. Even those who dismissed such talk could not deny that foreign enemies, unknown even to the king, might have attacked the capital under the cover of darkness.

In any case, an investigation got underway for several reasons: first, to protect the nation—England was at war with Holland, after all, and the government had a responsibility to investigate tales of enemy agents; second, to put to rest people's suspicions about prophesies of destruction; and third, no doubt, to ease the consciences of those stung by the *London Gazette's* accusation that "if the whole industry of the inhabitants had been applied to the stopping of the fire, and not to the saving of their particular *Goods,* the success might have been much better."

The authorities threw a wide net in hauling in suspects: "Diverse strangers, Dutch and French, were, during the fire, apprehended, upon suspicion that they contributed mischievously to it," reported the *Gazette*. They were given a "severe inquisition" by the Chief Justice and assisted by some of the lords of the Privy Council.

Several weeks after the fire, astrologer William Lilly received a summons to appear before the investigation committee. The order read, "That Mr. Lilly do attend this Committee on Friday next, being the 25th of October 1666 at two of the clock in the afternoon in Speaker's Chamber, to answer such Questions as shall be then and there asked him." He knew full well the reason for the summons, and it worried him.

Once already, he had taken credit for predicting a catastrophe. To his admirers, he had boasted that the

Rumors abounded of French and Dutch saboteurs setting the London fire in 1666; England was still at war with both countries. King Charles II made definite and bold proclamations against such a possibility in order to calm his countrymen, yet pursued inquiries into sabotage on his own.

plague of 1665 appeared in his 1651 almanac, *Monarchy or No Monarchy*. Now, during the six weeks following the Great Fire, he alleged that this second calamity had been another demonstration of his genius. Through astrology, he declared, he had foreseen England's worst fire. The evidence was right there in his book, contained in an illustration of "a great city all in flames of fire."

But this time, unfortunately, his eagerness to claim supernatural powers had landed him in serious trouble. During the course of the committee's investigation, a sinister coincidence involving William Lilly had surfaced. Six months earlier, in April, the government had unearthed a conspiracy to overthrow the king. Behind the plot was a group of officers still loyal to Oliver Cromwell, the Puritan leader who had successfully engineered the execution of the previous monarch, King Charles I. The *London Gazette*, reporting on the trial, revealed that a key part of the conspirators' plan was setting fire to London. During the pandemonium that would inevitably follow, they would seize power. The date chosen for the deed was September 3. Not only did that date mark the anniversary of two battlefield victories by Cromwell's forces, but also, the rebels, consulting William Lilly's almanac, *Monarchy or No Monarchy*, concluded that the horoscope for September 3—indeed, for the whole year 1666—seem to favor their schemes. At the conclusion of the trial, the conspirators' leader, a Colonel John Rathone, and eight fellow officers were pronounced guilty and executed. Now the committee examining London's destruction by fire wished to interview William Lilly, the man whose writings had inspired confidence in a band of traitors bent on arson.

In response to the summons, Lilly admitted that he felt timid around committees, understating his fear. He said his reluctance to appear was because some committees had insulted, scolded, criticized, and even mocked him. Nevertheless, he complied as ordered, but not without taking reinforcements. His influential friend Lord Ashmole accompanied him to the meeting. Even before the questioning began, Ashmole urged the committee members, recalled Lilly gratefully, "[to] befriend me and not permit me to be affronted or have any disgraceful language cast upon me."

Sir Robert Brooke addressed the astrologer first. "Mr. Lilly, this committee thought fit to summon you to appear before them this day to know if you can say any thing as to the cause of the late Fire, or whether there might be any designs therein. You are called the rather hither because in a book of yours, long since printed, you hinted some such thing by one of your hieroglyphics."

By way of background, Lilly rambled a bit about the circumstances in 1651 when the almanac was published. He reminded the committee that at the time the king was dead, peace was nowhere in sight, and the nation was in turmoil. His book, he said, was meant to be a scholar's glimpse of a possible future, hidden in pictures and charts that only educated people would understand.

One of the members grew impatient. "Did you foresee the year [of the fire]?" he asked.

"I did not," Lilly replied, apparently willing to throw overboard his reputation as a prophet if it could save his neck. Then, attempting to show his concern, he said he had looked into causes for the fire himself, but "I conclude that it was the only Finger of God, but what instruments He used thereunto, I am ignorant." In sum, he did not know more than anyone else why things happened in the world, although he had built his career on claiming that he did.

The committee, satisfied by Lilly's answers, dismissed him. "*Exit Lillius*," wrote Lilly at the end of his account of the interview—a stage direction for himself as if he were an actor in an important drama.

Meanwhile, the committee continued its hunt for suspects. Finally, it concluded its work by announcing that a culprit had been arrested. The government charged a 26-year-old French silversmith, Robert Hubert, with setting London on fire.

Hubert was a sad case, an example of someone who

sought fame by posing as a dangerous spy; or perhaps he was just a victim of his own imagination. His fellow workers testified that he was unbalanced. Pepys described him as a "mopish, besotted [drunken] fellow." According to Hubert at his trial, he and an accomplice passed a fire-ball—an explosive device—through a window of baker Farrinor's house in Pudding Lane on a long pole. When Farrinor said there was no such window, Hubert changed his story. He raised the number of accomplices to 23, which he later reduced to 3. He was taken to what was left of the shop in Pudding Lane and correctly identified it, which may have been his final undoing. The court sentenced him to hang, and he was marched out to the gallows at Tyburn. With the snap of the hangman's rope, the case of who set the Great Fire of London was officially closed.

Sir Christopher Wren (1632–1723) shows King Charles II the plan for rebuilding St. Paul's Cathedral. Although his scheme for rebuilding the entire city was deemed too costly, he was awarded the job of designing London's public buildings, including its churches.

Out of the Ashes

"Reader, if you seek a monument, look about you."

—words above the tomb of Sir Christopher Wren

E ven before Robert Hubert met his fate on the end of a rope at Tyburn, King Charles II was already deep into reviewing plans for rebuilding London. Within days of the fire, drawings for the layout of a new city had arrived, sent either directly to the king or to the Royal Society, the association of leading thinkers to which John Evelyn belonged. Between September 10 and September 20, Sir Christopher Wren, Evelyn himself, Robert Hooke, and Valentine Knight submitted their original plans for consideration. A fifth designer, Robert Newcourt, also submitted a plan, but there is no record of the date.

Christopher Wren, an inventor, professor of astronomy, and mathematician (Sir Isaac Newton credited him with helping Newton develop his theory of gravity), had been in Rome just three years before studying classical architecture. For Charles II, he produced a sweeping vision of how a redesigned London could take on the dimensions of a timeless city. His plans called for broad boulevards, open squares, and monumental buildings.

John Evelyn laid out a geometric grid for a new city, emphasizing intersections where the distinctiveness of public buildings would give each crossroads its own character.

Robert Hooke, a public works surveyor with a preference for order, put long east/west and north/south thoroughfares through the city to help move traffic, while adding small piazzas and islands to create quiet places for the populace.

Valentine Knight, an army officer, submitted a rather amateurishly drawn design with a printed explanation. His goal was to break up congested areas. Unfortunately, he suggested that the king could save money by rebuilding the city this way, diverting the money to finance the military instead. For assuming that His Majesty would be interested in profiting by his subjects' suffering, Knight was thrown into prison. He had survived both the plague and fire of London only to be incarcerated for offending the king!

Robert Newcourt, about whom not much is known, created a citywide design based on a simple principle: order of importance. Public buildings used by most people received central locations served by major thoroughfares. Parish churches, on the other hand, would be placed in the center of the neighborhoods they

Oliver Cromwell had usurped political, social, and religious power from King Charles I in 1649. A few months before the 1666 Great Fire of London, supporters of the then-dead opposition leader were discovered to be plotting to over-throw the king again.

served, accessible by small streets. His plan would produce large, medium, and small communities.

Interestingly, all the plans had several key features in common: they called for the removal of crooked streets, dead ends, narrow passageways, and hidden courtyards. This suggests that Londoners of the 17th century did not find the little lanes, alleys, and turn-arounds of their medieval city as charming as tourists do today.

Charles II studied the plans—although rejecting Knight's immediately—and made a decision. Sir Christopher Wren's was the most appealing, but it was much too costly. As a compromise, the king appointed Wren to be in charge of redesigning public buildings destroyed by the fire, with the assistance of Robert Hooke as surveyor. London's tangle of streets, however, would remain largely unchanged, as citizens began rebuilding immediately on their own.

King Charles II did make one important change to the composition of the city. He ordered that new houses be constructed of brick instead of timber and plaster. (The replica of Shakespeare's Globe Theater, erected in the mid-1990s, is the first building in London to have a thatched roof since 1666.) Charles also proposed fire prevention and building control legislation that regulated distances between buildings.

A large number of Londoners, however, driven from their homes and places of business by the fire, never returned to the city center. Merchants, in particular, relocated to the fashionably new West End where attractive residential neighborhoods were going up, such as Bloomsbury and Mayfair. Another change was the rise in popularity of coffeehouses, which became the chief sources of news and the seedbed of London's community of journalists, writers, and politicians, replacing in importance the old livery company halls representing various professions. Plague, incidentally, never returned in force to London again, or after 1667 to any other location in England. Although the disappearance of plague from London is generally attributed to the Great Fire's destruction of both the rats and of their favored hiding places, such as alleys, shaded courtyards, and the walls of old wooden buildings, this does not explain why plague vanished from the rest of

the country. The exact reasons for the cessation of plague in England remain a mystery.

In reconfiguring the city's physical layout, local authorities combined more than 100 parishes, with the result that Wren conceived plans for 50 new churches, including his magnificent St. Paul's Cathedral, which took 35 years to complete. For his smaller houses of worship, Wren refused to rely on cookie-cutter

The northwest view of St. Paul's Cathedral as designed by Christopher Wren. He also drew plans for 50 other churches, in effect creating a whole new look for the city of London.

designs. The churches range in style from simple Dutch to ornate Gothic, but each one bears the marks of Wren's passion for classical style. Wren also built the Royal Hospital in Chelsea and designed parts of Kensington Palace, Greenwich Hospital, the Royal Observatory of Greenwich, the royal Naval College, Drury Lane Theater, and Hampton Court Palace. A plaque in St. Paul's above Wren's tomb memorializes his legacy to London, with words written by his son: *"Lector, si monumentum requiris, circumspice"* ("Reader, if you seek a monument, look about you").

Wren also designed a commemoration of the Great Fire itself—a column 212 feet high topped by a bronze urn issuing flames. The original plans called for a statue of Charles II instead of an urn, but the king declined the honor, fearing that people would associate him with disaster. Laid on its side, the monument would reach to the exact spot in Pudding Lane where the fire started. In 1831, these words blaming Catholics for the fire were removed from the base: "but Popish frenzy, which wrought such horrors, is not yet quenched."

Another legacy of the Great Fire is fire insurance. A year after the fire, Dr. Nicholas Barbon offered contracts in case of loss due to fire. In 1680, Dr. Barbon and his partners placed "fire marks"—metal plates stamped with policy numbers—on the homes and businesses they insured. Nailed to the second story, out of reach of pilferers, fire marks identified policyholders before the days when each building had a separate address. By the end of the 17th century, competing insurance companies organized their own fire brigades—the first professional firefighters.

Finally, a permanent legacy of the Great Fire lies here in the United States—the city of Philadelphia.

Assisting Samuel Pepys during the frantic four days of the Great Fire was his friend Sir William Penn. Penn, an aristocrat by birth, converted to Quakerism as a young man. Later, he prevailed upon the king to grant him property in the New World, which became the colony of Pennsylvania. (Penn was embarrassed by the name, but His Majesty insisted.)

Penn hoped his colony would subsist mainly on agriculture, but it became clear that a town for businesspeople would be necessary. He chose a site where the Delaware and Schuylkill Rivers meet—a good port surrounded by rich farmland. Having witnessed

Christopher Wren designed yet one more public structure, a monument of the Great Fire (center). This column, 212 feet tall, was topped with a bronze urn and flames. It stood near the spot in Pudding Lane where the fire began. Some results of the catastrophe were fire insurance, professional firefighters, and new building codes.

This painting depicts a 1681 meeting in which William Penn (left), a wealthy English Quaker, received a land grant in the form of Pennsylvania from King Charles II (right). Penn had observed a London rife with congestion and disease, and determined the port city of his colony would be vastly different.

the congestion in old London that made the city so susceptible to disease and fire, Penn set aside 10,000 acres for a town that would occupy only 1,200 acres. Encircling the town would be an enormous greenbelt, a concept that gave rise to the modern suburb. Inside the city, two intersecting 100-foot wide boulevards— Broad and High Streets—would divide the city into quadrants, yet another mark of the modern city. Each residential lot would have enough room for a garden. Penn may have been influenced by Robert Newcourt's design for London, which created small communities bounded by streets.

Penn's overall rectangular design for Philadelphia, with its wide boulevards and acres of green space, seemed revolutionary at the time. Today, an urban layout of that nature is considered standard. Having seen firsthand the horrors of London in 1665 and 1666, Penn said he envisioned his "greene towne" of Philadelphia as one "which will never be burnt, and always be wholesome."

Chronology

1350   The Black Death kills one-third of the population of Europe, 25 million people

1640   English Revolution begins, developing into war between the Puritan-led Parliament and the forces of King Charles I

1649   King Charles I arrested and executed; England declares a Commonwealth

1653–8   Oliver Cromwell rules as Lord Protector of the Commonwealth until his death

1660   King Charles II restored to the English throne

1661   Plagues erupts in Turkey

1663–4   Plague in the Netherlands claims 35,000 lives

1664   Privy Council imposes quarantine on ships coming from ports where plague has been reported. Only five deaths of plague in London are reported for the year

1665   *April:* Three deaths from plague in the London outskirts

        May: 43 deaths from plague in the London outskirts

        June: Roads leading out of London clogged by people fleeing the city; Lord Chamberlain orders the theaters closed; Charles II, his court, and most of the upper class leave London; Privy Council takes steps to prevent persons suspected of having plague from wandering about the city

        July: Number of deaths for the month totals 5,567

        August: Streets are deserted; number of deaths in one week exceeds 5,000

        September: Heavy rain douses the bonfires set in the streets to fumigate the city; plague deaths decline for a few days; an estimated 12,000 die in a single week; the death toll for the month is 30,899

        October–November: Number of plague deaths declines from 4,500 a week to under 1,000

December: Droves of Londoners return to the city

1666   *February:* Charles II and his court return to London

July: Plague deaths hover around 40-50 a week

September: Fire breaks out in the king's baker's shop in Pudding Lane and spreads to consume 13,000 homes and most of the principal buildings in the city center

1667   An act of the city council outlines measures for fire prevention

1667–80s London rebuilds

Bibliography

Books and Articles

Bartel, Roland, ed. *London in Plague and Fire*. Boston: D.C. Heath and Company, 1957.

Boulton, Jeremy. *Neighbourhood and Society: A London Suburb in the Seventeenth Century*. Cambridge: Cambridge University Press, 1987.

Bowsky, William M. *The Black Death: A Turning Point in History*. Chicago: Holt, Rinehart & Winston, 1971.

Champion, Justin, ed. *Epidemic Disease in London*. Centre for Metropolitan History Working Papers Series, No. 1, 1993.

Cowie, Leonard W. *Plague and Fire: London 1665-66*. New York: Putnam, 1970.

Defoe, Daniel. *A Journal of the Plague Year*. Harmondsworth: Penguin (Classics edition), 1986.

Gray, Peter. *Plague and Fire: The Story of London 1665-66*. New York: McGraw-Hill, 1967.

Gregg, Charles T. *Plague: An Ancient Disease in the Twentieth Century*. Albuquerque: University of New Mexico Press, 1985.

Hanson, Julienne. "Order and Structure in Urban Design: The Plan for the Rebuilding of London after the Great Fire of 1666." *Ekistics,* January 1, 1989.

Hearsey, John E. N. *London and the Great Fire*. London: Murray, 1965.

Leasor, Thomas James. *The Plague and the Fire*. London: Allen & Unwin, 1962.

Marks, Geoffrey. *The Medieval Plague: The Black Death of the Middle Ages*. New York: Doubleday, 1971.

McNeill, William. *Plagues and Peoples*. Garden City: Anchor Press, 1976.

Mullett, Charles F. *The Bubonic Plague and England*. Lexington, KY: University of Kentucky Press, 1956.

Bibliography

Porter, Stephen. *The Great Plague.* Gloucester, England: Sutton Publishing Limited, 1999.

Ross, Sutherland. *The Plague and the Fire of London.* London: Faber & Faber, 1965.

Shrewsbury, J. F. D. *A History of the Bubonic Plague in the British Isles.* New York: Cambridge University Press, 1970.

Williman, Daniel, ed. *The Black Death: The Impact of the Fourteenth Century Plague.* Binghamton, NY: State University of New York, 1977.

Ziegler, Phillip. *The Black Death.* Wolfeboro Falls, NH: Alan Sutton Publishing, 1991.

Websites

Britain Express
http://www.britainexpress.com/

Catalog of the Scientific Community: John Evelyn
http://es.rice.edu/ES/humsoc/Galileo/Catalog/Files/evelyn.html

The English Merlin: The World of William Lilly and the 17th Century Astrologers
www.skyhook.co.uk/merlin/mainframe.htm

GlosNet: A Brief History of the Fire Brigade
http://www.gloscc.gov.uk/pubserv/gcc/fire/history/index.htm

The Great Plague of London
www.liv.ac.uk/~evansjon/humanities/history/The%20Great%20Plague%20of%20London.htm

A History of London's Firefighters
www.jmccall.demon.co.uk/history/page2.htm

London.com
http://www.see-london.com/briefhistory.asp

St. Bartholomew's Hospital Archive and Museum
www.medmicro.mds.qmw.ac.uk/yersinia/Plague_history.html

Index

Index

Index

Picture Credits

Cover Photos: New Millennium Images (front cover); New Millennium Images (back cover)

CHARLES J. SHIELDS was formerly the chairman of the guidance department at Homewood-Flossmoor High School in Flossmoor, Illinois. He currently writes full time from his home in Homewood, Illinois, where he lives with his wife, Guadalupe, an elementary school principal.

JILL McCAFFREY has served for four years as national chairman of the Armed Forces Emergency Services of the American Red Cross. Ms. McCaffrey also serves on the board of directors for Knollwood—the Army Distaff Hall. The former Jill Ann Faulkner, a Massachusetts native, is the wife of Barry R. McCaffrey, who served in President Bill Clinton's cabinet as director of the White House Office of National Drug Control Policy. The McCaffreys are the parents of three grown children: Sean, a major in the U.S. Army; Tara, an intensive care nurse and captain in the National Guard; and Amy, a seventh grade teacher. The McCaffreys also have two grandchildren, Michael and Jack.

DATE DUE			
NOV 0 1 2002			
APR 0 9 2009			

MEMBER OF
CHAUTAUQUA-CATTARAUGUS
LIBRARY SYSTEM